Mediterranean Instant Pot Cookbook for Beginners

Simple and Delicious Instant Pot Recipes for Beginners on Mediterranean Diet

Ariana Duncan

Copyright © 2019 by Ariana Duncan

All rights reserved worldwide.

ISBN: 978-1672043601

This document is geared towards providing exact and reliable information in regard to the topic and issue covered. The publication is sold with the idea that the publisher is not required to render accounting, officially permitted, or otherwise, qualified services. If advice is necessary, legal or professional, a practiced individual in the profession should be ordered.

From a Declaration of Principles which was accepted and approved equally by a Committee of the American Bar Association and a Committee of Publishers and Associations.

In no way is it legal to reproduce, duplicate, or transmit any part of this document in either electronic means or in printed format. Recording of this publication is strictly prohibited and any storage of this document is not allowed unless with written permission from the publisher. All rights reserved.

The information provided herein is stated to be truthful and consistent, in that any liability, in terms of inattention or otherwise, by any usage or abuse of any policies, processes, or directions contained within is the solitary and utter responsibility of the recipient reader. Under no circumstances will any legal responsibility or blame be held against the publisher for any reparation, damages, or monetary loss due to the information herein, either directly or indirectly.

Respective authors own all copyrights not held by the publisher.

Contents

INTRODUCTION **6**

BREAKFAST & BRUNCH **12**
Greek-Style Berry Yogurt 12
Chicken Panini 12
Spanish-Style Horchata 13
Tuna & Olive Salad 13
Cheesy Kale Frittata 13
Nutty Beef Steak Salad 14
Sage Soft-Boiled Eggs 14
Turkish Hard-Boiled Eggs 14
Spring Egg Salad 15
Mayo Spicy Deviled Eggs 15
Ground Beef & Cheese Scrambled Eggs 15
Potato & Egg Salad with Greek Yogurt 16
Garlic & Bell Pepper Frittata 16
Caprese Scrambled Eggs 16
Italian Ricotta & Tomato Omelet 17
Eggs with Spinach & Nuts 17
Spicy Poached Eggs with Mushrooms 17
Zesty Green Bites 18
Buttered Leeks with Poached Eggs 18
Cheesy Broccoli & Bell Pepper Frittata 18
Funghi & Aglio Pizza 19
Pizza Quattro Formaggi 19
Feta Turkey Meatballs with Tomato Sauce 20
Herbed Garlic Shrimp 20
Spinach Poached Egg Pancakes 20
Tasty Meatballs with Dilled Yogurt Dip 21
Green Onions Steamed Eggs 21
Tangy Cheesy Arancini 21

SOUPS & SAUCES **22**
Traditional Minestrone 22
Cream of Mushroom & Spinach Soup 22
Andalusian Lentil Soup 23
Bean & Zucchini Soup 23
Jalapeño Green Sauce 23
Parsley Garden Vegetable Soup 24
Chorizo Sausage & Fire-Roasted Tomato Soup 24
Lamb & Spinach Soup 24
Turkish Leek & Potato Soup 25
Classic Bolognese Sauce 25
Power Green Soup 25
Italian Broccoli & Potato Soup 26
Spanish Fall Soup 26
Broccoli Soup with Gorgonzola 26
Maltese Chickpea & Carrot Soup 26
Creamy Asparagus Soup 27

Old-Fashioned Chicken Soup 27
White Bean Pomodoro Soup 27
Feta-Topped Potato Gazpacho 28
Classic Napoli Sauce 28
Effortless Chicken Rice Soup 28

GRAINS & PASTA **29**
Spanish Chorizo & Spicy Lentils Stew 29
Moroccan Chicken & Chickpea Stew 29
Asparagus & Shrimp Risotto 30
Garbanzo Beans with Pancetta 30
Rice & Olives Stuffed Mushrooms 30
Pasta Shells Filled with Ricotta & Spinach 31
Chili-Garlic Rice with Halloumi 31
Cannellini Bean Stew with Spinach 32
Creamy Grana Padano Risotto 32
Rigatoni with Sausage and Spinach 32
Turkey Tortiglioni 33
Risoni with Carrots & Onion 33
Crispy Feta with Roasted Butternut Squash & Rice .. 34
Veggie Arborio Rice Bowls with Pesto 34
Simple Carnaroli Rice 34
Rice Stuffing Zucchini Boats 35
Easy Spanish Rice 35
Chard & Mushroom Risotto with Pumpkin Seeds 35
Cherry Tomato-Basil Linguine 36
Beef-Stuffed Pasta Shells 36
Pasta Caprese Ricotta-Basil Fusilli 36
Chicken Ragù Bolognese 37
Squash Parmesan & Linguine 37
Pork Spaghetti with Spinach and Tomatoes 38
Gouda Beef Fettuccine 38
Minestrone with Pesto & Rigatoni 38
Creamy Primavera Farfalle 39
Quattro Formaggi Tagliatelle 39

POULTRY **40**
Thyme Chicken with Veggies 40
Chicken with Tomatoes & Capers 40
Herby Chicken with Asparagus Sauce 41
Greek-Style Chicken with Potatoes 41
Lettuce Chicken Wraps 42
Paprika Buttered Chicken 42
Spicy Salsa Chicken with Feta 42
Chicken Cacciatore 43
Creamy Chicken Pasta with Pesto Sauce 43
Pesto Stuffed Chicken with Green Beans 44
Italian Chicken Thighs with Mushrooms 44
Chicken in Orange Gravy 44
Turkey with Rigatoni 45

Greek Turkey Meatballs 45
Chicken with Salsa Verde 46
Chicken Meatballs in Tomato Sauce 46
Chicken with Steamed Artichokes 46
Valencian Chicken Paella 47
Hot Chicken with Black Beans 47
Chicken Risotto with Vegetables 48
Spicy Mushroom Chicken 48
Mediterranean Chicken 48
Herbed Chicken Thighs 49
Lemon & Mustard Chicken 49
Italian-Style Turkey with Vegetables 50
Turkey Patties 50
Turkey Pepperoni Pizza 50
Roast Turkey with Basil and Garlic 51
Italian-Style Chicken Stew 51
Chicken in Garlic Yogurt Sauce 51

PORK 52

Pork Chops & Broccoli with Gravy 52
Italian Sausage & Cannellini Stew 52
Sausage with Celeriac & Potato Mash 53
Pork Chops with Squash Purée & Mushroom Gravy 53
Italian Tomato Glazes Pork Meatloaf 54
Pork & Mushroom Stew 54
Fennel Pork Estofado 54
Honey-Mustard Pork Chops 55
Jalapeño Pork 55
Dinner Pork Roast 55
Basil-Flavored Pork Stew 56
Pork Roast with Mushrooms Sauce 56
Pork Chops with Mushrooms in Tomato Sauce 56
Beans with Pancetta, Kale & Chickpeas 57
Pork Cutlets with Baby Carrots 57
Pork Sausage with Bell Peppers & Sweet Onions 57
Spicy Ground Pork 58
Marinated Flank Steak 58
Sweet & Sour Pork 59
Pork Fillets with Tomato Sauce 59

BEEF & LAMB 60

Beef with Garbanzo Beans 60
Beef & Bacon Chili 60
Brisket Chili con Carne 61
Beef Stew with Veggies 61
Beef and Pumpkin Stew 62
Greek Beef Gyros 62
Beef Stew with Eggplant & Parmesan 62
Meatloaf & Cheesy Mashed Potatoes 63
Beef & Vegetable Stew 63
Italian-Style Pot Roast 64
Meatballs with Marinara Sauce 64
Crispy Beef with Rice 64

Short Ribs with Mushroom & Asparagus Sauce 65
Beef & Mushroom Steaks 65
Beef Stew with Green Peas 66
Italian Beef Sandwiches with Pesto 66
Italian-Style Calf's Liver 66
Rosemary Meatloaf 67
Peppery Beef 67
Lemony Lamb Stew 67
Beef & Eggplant Casserole 68
Beef Stuffed Red Peppers 68
Beef & Rice Stuffed Onions 68
Sour Potato Beef Lasagne 69
Eggplant Stew with Almonds 69
Classic Italian Lamb Ragout 70
Garlic & Pancetta Lamb Leg 70
Sesame Lamb 70

FISH & SEAFOOD 71

Steamed Mediterranean Cod 71
Steamed Sea Bass with Turnips 71
Salmon with Dill Chutney 72
Spanish Chorizo & Shrimp Boil 72
Cod in Lemon-Sweet Sauce 72
Spicy Tangy Salmon with Rice 73
Shrimp with Brussels Sprouts 73
White Wine Mussels 74
Paella Señorito 74
Buttery Herb Trout with Green Beans 74
Cod on Millet 75
Potato Chowder with Hot Shrimp 75
Prawn & Clam Paella 76
Haddock Fillets with Crushed Potatoes 76
Seafood Spicy Penne 76
Shrimp Farfalle with Spinach 77
Mussel Chowder with Oyster Crackers 77
Crabmeat with Asparagus & Broccoli Pilaf 78
Italian Salmon with Creamy Polenta 78
Orange Salmon Fillets 78
Garlic-Lemon Salmon Steak 79
Crispy Herbed Trout 79
Garlicky Seafood Pasta 79
Green Mackerel with Potatoes 80
Herbs & Lemon Stuffed Tench 80
Quick Salmon Fillets 80
Fish Stew 81
Lemon & Dill Salmon with Greens 81
Marinated Squid in White Wine Sauce 81
Octopus & Shrimp with Collard Greens 82
Anchovy & Mussel Rice 82
Steamed Sea Bream 82
Rosemary & Dill Trout Fillet 83
Red Pollock & Tomato Stew 83
Squid Ink Pasta with Trout Fillets 83

Marinated Smelt with Mustard Rice 84
Thick Fish Soup 84
White Wine Catfish Fillets 84
Trout & Spinach with Tomato Sauce 85
Tuna & Rosemary Pizza 85
Chili & Oregano Salmon Fillet 86
Garlic Seafood with Brown Rice 86
Citrusy Marinated Grilled Catfish 86

VEGETABLES & VEGAN 87

Green Minestrone 87
Vegan Carrot Gazpacho 87
Green Beans with Feta & Nuts 87
Garlic Veggie Mash with Parmesan 88
Pesto Arborio Rice Bowls with Veggies 88
Italian Vegetable Stew 88
Mashed Potatoes with Spinach 89
Herby-Garlic Potatoes 89
Mushroom & Rice Stuffed Bell peppers 89
Steamed Artichokes with Lemon Aioli 90
Artichoke with Garlic Mayo 90
Green Lasagna Soup 90
Rosemary Sweet Potato Medallions 91
Asparagus with Feta 91
Quick Greek Dolmades 91
Potato Balls in Marinara Sauce 92
Arugula Pizza 92
Eggplant Lasagna 93
Spinach and Leeks with Goat Cheese 93
Colorful Vegetable Medley 93
Sweet Chickpea & Mushroom Stew 94
Vegetarian Paella 94
Vegetable Stew 94
Stewed Kidney Bean 95
Lentil Spread with Parmesan 95
Broccoli & Orecchiette Pasta with Feta 95
Mushroom & Spinach Cannelloni 96
Mushroom Spinach Tagliatelle 96
Feta Cheese Stuffed Potatoes 96
Leek & Garlic Cannellini Beans 97
Mushroom & Vegetable Penne Pasta 97
Braised Swiss Chard with Potatoes 97

DESSERTS 98

Cinnamon Apple Crisp 98
Dark Chocolate Brownies 98
Cinnamon Pumpkin Pudding 98
Flan with Whipping Cream 99
Nutmeg Squash Tart 99
Warm Winter Apple Compote 100
Vanilla Apple Tart 100
Chocolate & Banana Squares 100
Yogurt Cake with Chocolate Glaze 101

Savoury Lemon Dessert 101
Honey Crema Catalana 102
Marble Cherry Cake 102
Simple Apricot Dessert 102
Stewed Plums with Almond Flakes 103
Vanilla & Walnut Cake 103
Vanilla Sweet Tortillas 103
Pumpkin & Walnut Sweet Rolls 104
Cinnamon & Lemon Apples 104

Introduction

Hello! Welcome to my book of Mediterranean recipes for the Instant Pot.

My recipes are simply too delicious to keep to myself. And it's the only cookbook you'll need to make the most delicious Instant Pot recipes you've ever tasted!

If there's one kitchen appliance I can't live without, it's my Instant Pot. This gadget has changed my life completely in the kitchen! Gone are the days when I spent hrs each week, prepping and then cooking meals. And so many times those meals were tasteless, with leftovers that no one wanted to eat.

Then along came my Instant Pot Pressure Cooker… and now I make delectable meals every day. Quick cooking, tasty recipes - and I have leftovers my family fights and squabbles over! Like the juiciest pork shoulders and spicy rice dishes. In my book, you'll find a collection of mouthwatering and flavorsome recipes from every cuisine.

One of the biggest appealing features of the Instant Pot is that it makes fresh and fast homey meals in no time. Whether you're vegetarian or love your meat and chicken, my book has the best recipes for making amazing, healthy meals. And make sure you make an extravagant cheat recipe on those days when you're not counting Cal and fat! Those are the best recipes of all.

In this book, I share my favorite recipes with you, and I'll help you get familiar with the Instant Pot, so you know exactly how to use one. Breakfasts, appetizers, Sunday dinners, and delightfully sweet desserts! I have just the recipe for you.

So now, let's learn all about the Instant Pot so you can start cooking!

WHAT IS AN INSTANT POT PRESSURE COOKER?

Now that you know how much I love my Instant Pot, you'll want to know just what an electric Pressure cooker is. The Instant Pot is an appliance that's a combination of a pressure cooker, slow cooker, rice cooker, and yogurt maker – all in one handy kitchen device.

What parts make up the Instant Cooker? There's an outer pot, which is the base and heat source of the Pressure cooker. Inside of this outer pot goes the inner pot, which is made from durable stainless steel. This inner pot is where all the cooking happens. There's a lid that goes on top of the inner pot, which has a Silicone ring that Seals tightly to keep food, liquids, and Pressure securely in the pot.

On top of the lid are the Pressure release and the float valve. The Pressure release does just that – it releases Pressure from inside the Instant Pot. The float valve on the lid pops up when the Instant Pot is Pressurized and lowers back down when it's not. You'll know it's safe to open the lid when the float valve is down.

The Instant Pot has a condensation collector on the side of the base unit that can be Removed. Its purpose is to collect condensation, usually when the Instant Pot is being used as a slow cooker.

Depending on the model of Instant Pot you have, it may come with some useful accessories – a steaming rack, measuring cup, and a set of spoons.

Not a complex appliance at all, right?

Get to know your brand of Instant Pot by taking a few minutes to read the instruction manual. Even though all electric pressure cookers have pretty much the same functions and settings, every brand comes with some unique features.

IS THE MEDITERRANEAN DIET HEALTHY?

I'm going to let you in on a little secret. Most popular healthy diets that are touted for weight loss—from Paleo to Whole 30 to Clean Eating to Mediterranean and Vegetarian—share the same principles.

They involve consuming whole foods (contrary to packaged and processed) and bringing in some quality protein, healthy fats, complex carbs, fiber and mineral-rich veggies to your plate. However, each of these diets presents you a marginally different path that leads to fulfilling these principles.

That's why I'll be breaking them down for you one so you can figure out which one (if any!) is right for you. I'll also quickly explain the facts and provide you with quick and actionable tips on how to follow the Mediterranean diet as part of a healthy and nutritious life.

The Why

The Mediterranean Diet is inspired by the traditional diets of the people who live in the Mediterranean sea, most precisely Greece, Italy, Spain, and France. It's formed on plant-based foods like vegetables and fruits, grains, nuts, legumes and plenty of olive oil, fresh fish and seafood.

What You Can Eat

A lot of fresh veggies, some fruit, whole grains such as brown rice, beans, and some nuts. Fish, seafood, and chicken are the protein pillars, especially if flavored with some fresh herbs and spices. Dairy is consumed occasionally in the shape of fresh cheeses, eggs, and yogurt, or as a part of the loving latte mmmmh! While pasta is an entry, it's commonly consumed in small portions at the beginning of a meal, and it's usually fresh.

Picture a vibrant Italian salad with greens, juicy tomatoes, cucumbers, and fresh mozzarella, topped with herbs and a piece of grilled chicken, fish or shrimp.

What You Can't Eat

Usually, you are to avoid packaged, or processed foods made with some form of added sugar or refined grains and oils. Red meat is also a choice that has to be limited - to a few times per month. Butter, ghee or canola oil should be limited as well, though I recommend them for frying as the extra-virgin olive oil is not the best.

Pros & Cons

The basics of Mediterranean diet mimic the basic principles of healthy nutrition: whole foods and grains, tons of vegetables, seasonal fruits, and healthy fats. (Win-Win-Win!)

Its health benefits are also the most well-documented (seriously) by research studies. It's particularly powerful when it comes to heart health. It's been linked to lowering heart disease risk factors like high LDL cholesterol levels and high blood sugar and to reducing heart attacks and death from heart disease. The diet may also protect your brain as you age.

Tip: the Mediterranean Diet emphasizes the importance of enjoying meals with family and friends (and a nice bottle of red wine), which also comes with some additional mental health benefits.

The only con I can think of is that it may be difficult to do while trying to eat seasonally and locally depending on where you are, and some of the pros may differ from the Mediterranean lifestyle. Try not to overdo it: it's very easy to go a forget on the portion size when eating juicy olives and fresh cheese while having red wine.

BENEFITS OF COOKING WITH THE INSTANT POT

Nutritious meals

Pressure cooking, slow cooking, and steaming foods keep in flavor and nutrients and create delicious and moist dishes. The recipes in my book use all of these functions.

Save time and energy

Using the Instant Pot saves you a lot of time. You can eat healthy at home, without spending the time you don't have, prepping and then cooking your meals. And fast cooking = energy saving. Cooking with your Instant pot is fast and efficient, cutting down your electricity bill by cooking in less time than you would on the stovetop or in the oven.

Pick your size

Most Instant Pots models come in three convenient sizes: 3, 6, and 8-quart. For most families, 6-quart is the right size. The 3-quart mini Instant Pot is perfect for when you want to cook a small meal or a small amount of pasta or rice. And the 8-quart works for large families, or if you just like to make extra meals for another time. I've included recipes in my book that you can double so you can freeze mouthwatering meals for lunches and dinner.

No more mad-rush cooking

How often have you had no time at all to even think about what you're making for dinner? Those days of panic are over. Your Instant Pot is there for you! There are some fast and easy meals included in the recipe book that in just minutes help you get a fantastic dinner on the table.

Hot breakfast!

Tired of waking up to cold cereal as your only breakfast option? Your Instant Pot can make hot oatmeal in minutes. Or make breakfast in your Instant Pot the night before and just Heat up in the morning.

Cook perfect rice every time!

Make rice in your electric pressure cooker, and you'll never go back to making it stove-top again. White, Brown, or basmati – some people would say the Instant Pot was made for rice.

Even Heating

Heat is evenly distributed in the Instant Pot. This means everything is cooked at the same time and is done to the same perfection.

Time your meals

Because of the Instant Pot cooks so fast, use the Delay Start function to time your meals, so they're ready when you get home. Many of my recipes let you prep your food the night before and then put them in the Instant Pot on the timer, cooking them to perfection every time.

The handy "Keep Warm" function

Most Instant Pot models will have a Keep Warm function. When cooking is done, Keep Warm will turn on, so your meal is ready, warm, and waiting for whenever you're ready to sit down and eat.

HOW TO USE THE INSTANT POT

When you first get your Instant Pot don't be intimidated by all the buttons, functions, and programs. That's what my recipe book is for – to guide you through the steps of using an electric pressure cooker with no confusion. Here are some basic things about your Instant Pot that can make it easy for you to start cooking.

Just what is pressure cooking?

Let's get some of the technical information out of the way so you can get to the good stuff… the recipes! The Instant Pot uses a cooking method that seals ingredients and liquids inside a sealed pot. It uses heat to create steam, which then builds up the pressure in the pot. This steam is released or trapped in the pot to control the amount of pressure. The more pressure there is, the higher the temperature – and the faster food cooks. Sound complex? All you really need to know is that your Instant Pot cooks food fast, fast, fast!

Water test before first use

I know you'll be anxious to find a recipe and start cooking right away but take a few minutes to set up your Instant Pot and do a water pressure test. This is a great way to get familiar with how an electric pressure cooker works. Just Pour 2 to 3 cups of water into the Instant Pot. Lock the lid and seal. Choose a setting with a short time or use the Manual button and set for 5 minutes. Then watch the magic happen. The water will first heat until pressure is built up. When high pressure is reached cooking begins, and the time on the Instant Pot will start counting down.

Instant Pot settings

Those buttons may look complicated, with a different button for each different program. Don't worry; it won't take you long to understand which ones to Press. To simplify it – depending on your brand of Instant Pot, each button refers to its methods of cooking, such as the Rice function or the Poultry function.

Releasing Pressure

Releasing Pressure is easy. When you want to lower the temperature, or stop cooking altogether, use either the Natural Release or the quick release. The easy way is to use the Natural Release, where you don't do anything at all. When the cooking cycle is complete just wait until the pressure drops on its own before opening the pot. This can take between 10 to 30 minutes depending on the amount of food and liquid in the pot.

Use the quick release when you want to release steam quickly to stop cooking, so food isn't overcooked. This method of pressure release is great for foods such as fish and vegetables. To do a quick release turn the valve on the lid of the instant pot from the "Sealing" position to "venting."

Cleaning the Instant Pot

Ah… clean up is nice and easy with an electric pressure cooker. For daily cleaning, just wipe the outside of the outer pot and clean the rim as well. I recommend using a soft foam brush for the rim. Clean the inside pot, either by hand, or you can toss it in the dishwasher with the rest of your dinner dishes. Some of the little parts, such as the pressure release on the lid, can get sticky so remember to wipe them down.

Safety tips

Your Instant Pot is completely safe to use, but as with any kitchen appliance there are a few safety tips to keep in mind:

Always follow instructions for releasing pressure from the pot. For fatty cuts of meat use the Natural Release method to avoid a burn from splattering hot fat.

Never use force to take off the lid.

Avoid using more than ¼ cup of oil or other fat in a recipe.

MY TOP 5 INSTANT POT TIPS AND TRICKS TO MAKE AMAZING FOOD!

1. The Friendly, Dried Bean

Using canned beans can get pricey if you're using a lot of them in soups and stews. The Instant Pot can cook dried beans in less than an hr, much faster than the 3 to 4 hrs it takes to cook them on the stove. Using your electric pressure cooker, you can buy a variety of dried beans and have them on hand to make many of the delicious meals in my cookbook.

2. Creamy, Rich Yogurt

Eat a lot of yogurts? The Instant Pot is perfect for making low fat or creamy, rich yogurt. You'll save a lot of money by making your own. It's much tastier than the store bought yogurt! And you can use it in my recipes.

3. Don't Forget the Sauté Function!

An often-overlooked function of your electric pressure cooker is the Sauté Function. Use this setting to Brown, Sauté, and simmer meat and other ingredients, such as onions. Sautéing gives recipes a richness that infuses your meals with flavor.

4. Avoid Messy Clean sup

Use the Natural Release, or as I call it the "do nothing release", to avoid messy clean up in your kitchen. Dishes that have a lot of liquid, such as soups, can move around a lot in the pot if you use the quick release, resulting in spills. Using the Natural Release means there less movement of liquid in the pot, so less clean up. And more time for you to read through my book for your next recipe!

5. Buy a Second Instant Pot!

Buy an Instant Pot for yourself… and an extra one as a gift. Because when your family and friends taste the great meals that come out of your kitchen, they're going to want to know how you're doing it. And when you share with them that it's my recipe book behind your delicious dinners, they'll want an Instant Pot of their own.

MY INSTANT POT RECIPES

Ready to use your Instant Pot? I've created some great recipes for my Instant Pot, and now I'm sharing them with you. These recipes are easy to follow… and the result is delicious!

Before you start cooking, let's take a look at some of the basics for using my recipes for the Instant Pot, basics that will make it easier for you to jump right in and make some great meals.

What can you cook in your Instant Pot?

Any foods that you usually cook in a liquid can be cooked in the Instant Pot, such as beans, rice, risotto, soups, and stews. Chicken and meats are great cooked in an electric pressure cooker, so long as you don't want them to be crispy. And don't forget your vegetables. Steam broccoli, green beans, and cauliflower. Harder vegetables such as carrots, onions, and potatoes cook nicely in the pressure cooker.

Essential functions you need to know

There are a few basic functions that your Instant Pot can perform, all of which are used in my recipes:

Pressure Cook/Manual: Foods that take a long time for the flavors to blend are best cooked using the Pressure Cooker method. Roasts prepared this way are great – juicy, tender, and full of flavor.

Sauté: This function lets the bottom of the pot Sauté and sear foods first. Then you can pressure cook them. This gives foods a nice deep flavor.

Slow Cook: Use the Slow Cook function for tough cuts of meat that need to cook for a long time as well as for meals that you want to simmer for a few hrs, such as beef stew.

Steam: You can steam foods using the steamer rack that comes with your Instant Pot. This is good for foods such as vegetables when you don't want to cook them in a liquid where they become soggy.

Use enough liquid

The Instant Pot uses steam to build up the pressure so food cooks. My recipes will let you know how much liquid to use, but as a rule, most recipes for the electric pressure cooker will need 1 to 2 cups of liquid. If you're cooking meat that is juicy, you can lower the liquid amount to a ½ cup.

Filling the Instant Pot

When you're using your Instant Pot for pressure cooking, never fill it more than halfway. If there are too much liquid and food in the pot, hot liquid can come spraying out of the release valve and cause burns.

Using frozen is okay

You don't need to remember to take food out of the freezer to use for your evening meal. The Instant Pot cooks frozen foods with no problems. I use frozen fruit and vegetables in many of my recipes – they defrost and then cook perfectly.

Dessert, dessert, and more dessert

If you don't use your Instant Pot to make desserts and other sweets, you'll be missing out! In my house, dessert is a big deal. Cakes, pies, even apple crisp. All types of yummy desserts are possible in your Instant Pot! I've included some of my favorite dessert recipes in this book.

People all over the world have fallen for the Instant Pot, and now you can too! My tips, tricks, and recipes for using your Instant Pot are all you need to make delicious meals that you and your family won't be able to get enough of.

The recipes in this book are the ones I make over and over again. Not only are these recipes easy to make, but they're also delicious and full of flavor. Look through my recipes and find one that catches your eye. Then send out the invitations to your first Instant Pot dinner!

BREAKFAST & BRUNCH

Greek-Style Berry Yogurt

Servings: 12 | Prep + Cook Time: 23 hours 20 minutes

INGREDIENTS

1 pound hulled and halved raspberries
1 cup sugar
3 tbsp gelatin
1 tbsp fresh orange juice
8 cups milk
¼ cup Greek yogurt containing active cultures

DIRECTIONS

In a bowl, mash raspberries with a potato masher. Add sugar and stir well to dissolve; let soak for 30 minutes at room temperature. Add in lemon juice and gelatin and mix well until dissolved.

Remove the mixture and place in a sealable container, close, and allow to sit for 12 hrs to 24 hrs at room temperature before placing in a refrigerator. Refrigerate for a maximum of 2 weeks.

Into the cooker, add milk and close the lid. The steam vent should be set to Venting then to Sealing.

Select Yogurt until "Boil" is displayed on the readings. When complete there will be a display of "Yogurt" on the screen. Open the lid and using a food thermometer ensure the milk temperature is at least 185° F.

Transfer the steel pot to a wire rack and allow cool for 30 minutes until milk has reached 110° F.

In a bowl, mix ½ cup warm milk and yogurt. Transfer the mixture into the remaining warm milk and stir without having to scrape the steel pot's bottom.

Take the pot back to the base of the pot and seal the lid. Select Yogurt mode and cook for 8 hrs.

Allow the yogurt to chill in a refrigerator for 1-2 hrs.

Transfer the chilled yogurt to a large bowl and stir in fresh raspberry jam.

Chicken Panini

Servings: 4 | Prep + Cook Time: 45 minutes

INGREDIENTS

4 chicken thighs, boneless and skinless
Salt to taste
2 cups basil-tomato sauce
1 onion, minced
2 garlic cloves, minced
2 tbsp minced fresh parsley
1 tbsp lemon juice
1 tbsp mayonnaise
1½ cups iceberg lettuce, shredded
4 panini rolls

DIRECTIONS

Season the chicken with salt, and transfer into the pot. Add in garlic, onion and tomato-basil sauce. Coat the chicken by turning in the sauce. Seal the lid and Cook on High Pressure for 15 minutes.

Do a natural release for 10 minutes. Use two forks to shred the chicken and mix into the sauce. Press Keep Warm and let the mixture to simmer for 15 minutes to thicken the sauce, until desired consistency.

Meanwhile, in a bowl, mix lemon juice, mayonnaise, salt, and parsley; toss lettuce into the mixture to coat. Separate the chicken in equal parts to match the panini rolls; apply lettuce for topping and complete the sandwiches.

Spanish-Style Horchata

Servings: 6 | Prep + Cook Time: 20 minutes

INGREDIENTS

2 cups water
1 cup chufa seed, overnight soak
¼ stick cinnamon

Zest from 1 lemon
2 tbsp sugar
4 cups cold water

DIRECTIONS

In the pot, combine cinnamon, chufa seed and 4 cups water. Seal the lid cook on High Pressure for 1 minute. Release Pressure naturally for 10 minutes, then release the remaining Pressure quickly.

In a blender, add chufa seed mixture, lemon zest and sugar. Blend well to form a paste. Add 2 cups cold water into a large container. Strain the blended chufa mixture into the water. Mix well and place in the refrigerator until ready for serving. Add cinnamon stick for garnishing.

Tuna & Olive Salad

Servings: 4 | Prep + Cook Time: 15 minutes

INGREDIENTS

1½ pounds potatoes, quartered
2 eggs
3 tbsp melted butter
Salt and pepper to taste
6 pickles, chopped

2 tbsp red wine vinegar
½ cup pimento stuffed green olives
½ cup chopped roasted red peppers
2 tbsp chopped fresh parsley
10 ounces canned tuna, drained

DIRECTIONS

Pour 2 cups of water into the pot and add potatoes. Place a trivet over the potatoes. Lay the eggs on the trivet. Seal the lid and cook for 8 minutes on High Pressure. Do a quick release.

Drain and remove potatoes to a bowl. Transfer the eggs in filled with an ice water bowl. Drizzle melted butter over the potatoes and season with salt and pepper. Peel and chop the chilled eggs.

Add pickles, eggs, peppers, tuna, vinegar to the potatoes and mix to coat. Serve topped with olives.

Cheesy Kale Frittata

Servings: 6 | Prep + Cook Time: 20 minutes

INGREDIENTS

6 large eggs
2 tbsp heavy cream
½ tsp freshly grated nutmeg
Salt and ground black pepper to taste

1 ½ cups kale, chopped
¼ cup grated Parmesan Cheese
Cooking spray
1 cup water

DIRECTIONS

In a bowl, beat eggs, nutmeg, pepper, salt, and cream until smooth. Stir in Parmesan Cheese and kale.

Apply a cooking spray to a cake pan. Wrap aluminum foil around outside of the pan to cover completely.

Place egg mixture into the prepared pan. Pour in water, set a steamer rack over the water. Gently lay the pan onto the rack. Seal the lid and cook for 10 minutes on High Pressure. Release the pressure quickly.

Nutty Beef Steak Salad

Servings: 4 | Prep + Cook Time: 60 minutes

INGREDIENTS

1 lb rib-eye steak, boneless
4 oz fresh arugula
1 large tomato, chopped
¼ cup fresh goat's cheese
4 almonds
4 walnuts

4 hazelnuts
3 tbsp olive oil
2 cups beef broth
2 tbsp red wine vinegar
1 tbsp Italian Seasoning mix

DIRECTIONS

Whisk together vinegar, Italian mix, and olive oil. Brush each steak with this mixture and place in your instant pot. Pour in the broth and seal the lid.

Cook on Meat/Stew for 25 minutes on High Pressure. Release the Pressure naturally, for about 10 minutes, and remove the steaks along with the broth.

Grease the inner pot with oil and hit Sauté. Brown the steaks on both sides for 5-6 minutes. Remove from the pot and cool for 5 minutes before slicing.

In a bowl, mix arugula, tomato, cheese, almonds, walnuts, and hazelnuts. Top with steaks and drizzle with red wine mixture.

Sage Soft-Boiled Eggs

Servings: 4 | Prep + Cook Time: 15 minutes

INGREDIENTS

4 large eggs
1 cups water

Salt and ground black pepper, to taste
1 tbsp sage

DIRECTIONS

To the pressure cooker, add water and place a wire rack. Carefully place eggs on it. Seal the lid, press Steam and cook for 3 minutes on High Pressure. Do a quick release.

Allow to cool completely in an ice bath. Peel the eggs, in half lengthwise and season with sage, salt, and pepper before serving.

Turkish Hard-Boiled Eggs

Servings: 6 | Prep + Cook Time: 20 minutes

INGREDIENTS

1 ½ cups water
6 large eggs
1 tbsp paprika

1 tbsp butter, melted
Salt and black pepper to taste

DIRECTIONS

In the pot, add water and place a trivet. Lay your eggs on top. Seal the lid and cook for 5 minutes on High Pressure. Do a natural release for 10 minutes. Transfer the eggs to ice cold water to cool completely. Mix the butter with paprika. Pell en cut the eggs in half lengthwise. Season with salt and pepper, pour the paprika butter over and serve.

Spring Egg Salad

Servings: 6 | Prep + Cook Time: 30 minutes

INGREDIENTS

2 cups water
Cooking spray
6 eggs
¼ cup crème fraîche
2 large spring onions, minced
1 tbsp dill, minced
2 tsp mustard
salt and black pepper to taste

DIRECTIONS

Grease a cake pan with cooking spray. Carefully crack the eggs into the pan. To the inner pot, add water. Set pan on the trivet.

Seal the lid and cook for 5 minutes on High Pressure. Do a quick release. Loosen the eggs on the edges with a knife. Transfer to a cutting board and chop into smaller sizes.

Transfer the chopped eggs to a bowl. Add in onion, mustard, salt, dill, crème fraîche, and black pepper.

Mayo Spicy Deviled Eggs

Servings: 6 | Prep + Cook Time: 20 minutes

INGREDIENTS

1 cup water
10 large eggs
¼ cup cream cheese
¼ cup mayonnaise
Salt and ground black pepper to taste
¼ tsp chili powder

DIRECTIONS

Add water, insert the steamer basket and lay the eggs inside

Seal the lid and cook on High Pressure for 5 minutes. Release the Pressure quickly.

Drop eggs into an ice bath to cool for 5 minutes. Peel eggs and halve them.

Transfer yolks to a bowl and use a fork to mash; Stir in cream cheese, and mayonnaise. Add pepper and salt for seasoning. Ladle yolk mixture into egg white halves.

Ground Beef & Cheese Scrambled Eggs

Servings: 3 | Prep + Cook Time: 25 minutes

INGREDIENTS

6 oz lean ground beef
1 onion, chopped
6 eggs
¼ cup skim milk
¼ cup cottage cheese
¼ tsp garlic powder
¼ tsp rosemary powder
1 tbsp tomato paste
½ tsp sea salt
2 tbsp olive oil

DIRECTIONS

Grease the inner pot with olive oil. Stir-fry the onions, for 4 minutes, until translucent, on Sauté. Add beef and tomato paste. Cook for 5 minutes, stirring twice.

Meanwhile, Whisk the eggs, milk, cheese, rosemary, garlic, and salt. Pour the mixture into the pot and stir slowly with a wooden spatula. Cook until slightly underdone. Remove from the heat and serve.

Potato & Egg Salad with Greek Yogurt

Servings: 8 | Prep + Cook Time: 20 minutes

INGREDIENTS

1 ½ cups water
6 sweet potatoes, peeled and diced
4 large eggs
2 ½ cups mayonnaise
¼ cup dill, chopped
⅓ cup Greek yogurt
Salt and ground black pepper to taste
½ cup arugula

DIRECTIONS

Pour water. Place eggs and potatoes into the steamer basket; Transfer to the pot and seal the lid.

Cook for 4 minutes on High Pressure. Do a quick release.

Take out the eggs and place in a bowl of ice-cold water for purposes of cooling. In a bowl, combine yogurt, mayonnaise, and dill.

In a separate bowl, mash potatoes using a potato masher; mix with mayonnaise mixture to coat.

Skin and dice the eggs. Transfer to the potato salad and mix. Season to taste and serve.

Garlic & Bell Pepper Frittata

Servings: 2 | Prep + Cook Time: 20 minutes

INGREDIENTS

2 red bell peppers, chopped
4 eggs
2 tbsp olive oil
2 garlic cloves, crushed
1 tsp Italian Seasoning mix

DIRECTIONS

Grease the pot with oil. Stir-fry the peppers for 2-3 minutes, or until lightly charred. Set aside. Add garlic and stir-fry for 1 minute, until soft.

Whisk the eggs and season with Italian seasoning. Pour the mixture into the pot and cook for 2-3 minutes, or until set. Using a spatula, loosen the edges and gently slide onto a plate. Add charred peppers and fold over. Serve hot.

Caprese Scrambled Eggs

Servings: 2 | Prep + Cook Time: 25 minutes

INGREDIENTS

4 eggs
½ cup fresh mozzarella cheese
1 cup button mushrooms, chopped
1 large tomato, chopped
2 spring onions, chopped
¼ cup milk
2 tbsp olive oil
½ tsp salt

DIRECTIONS

Grease the pot with oil and set on Sauté. Stir-fry the onions for 3 minutes, or until translucent. Add tomatoes and mushrooms.

Cook until liquid evaporates, for 5-6 minutes. Meanwhile, Whisk eggs, cheese, milk, and salt. Pour into the pot and stir. Cook for 2 minutes, or until set.

Italian Ricotta & Tomato Omelet

Servings: 4 | Prep + Cook Time: 30 minutes

INGREDIENTS

1 lb tomatoes, peeled, roughly diced
1 tbsp tomato paste
1 tsp brown sugar
1 cup ricotta cheese
4 eggs

3 tbsp olive oil
1 tbsp Italian seasoning mix
¼ cup fresh parsley, chopped
¼ tsp salt

DIRECTIONS

Grease the inner pot with oil. Press Sauté and add tomatoes, sugar, Italian seasoning, parsley, and salt. Give it a good stir and cook for 15 minutes or until the tomatoes soften. Stir occasionally.

Meanwhile, whisk eggs and cheese. Pour the mixture into the pot stir well. Cook for 3 more minutes. Serve immediately.

Eggs with Spinach & Nuts

Servings: 4 | Prep + Cook Time: 25 minutes

INGREDIENTS

1 lb spinach, rinsed, chopped
3 tbsp olive oil
1 tbsp butter
1 tbsp almonds, crushed

1 tbsp peanuts, crushed
4 eggs
½ tsp chili flakes
½ tsp sea salt

DIRECTIONS

Pour 1 ½ cups of water into the inner pot and insert a steamer basket. Place the eggs onto the basket. Seal the lid and cook on High Pressure for 5 minutes.

Do a quick release. Remove the eggs to an ice bath. Wipe the pot clean, and heat oil on Sauté. Add spinach and cook for 2-3 minutes, stirring occasionally.

Stir in 1 tbsp of butter and season with salt and chili flakes. Mix well and cook for 1 more minute. Press Cancel and sprinkle with nuts. Peel and slice each egg in half, lengthwise. Transfer to a serving plate and pour over spinach mixture.

Spicy Poached Eggs with Mushrooms

Servings: 1 | Prep + Cook Time: 25 minutes

INGREDIENTS

3 oz button mushrooms, cut half lengthwise
2 oz fresh arugula
1 egg

2 tbsp olive oil
Chili flakes, for Seasoning

DIRECTIONS

Melt butter on Sauté, add mushrooms and cook for 4-5 minutes, until soft. Stir in arugula. Cook for one minute. Crack the egg and cook until set – for 2 minutes.

Season with chili flakes. Press Cancel and remove the omelet to a serving plate.

Zesty Green Bites

Servings: 8 | Prep + Cook Time: 45 minutes

INGREDIENTS

¼ cup frozen chopped kale
¼ cup finely chopped artichoke hearts
¼ cup ricotta cheese
2 tbsp grated Parmesan cheese
¼ cup goat cheese
1 large egg white
1 tsp dried basil
1 lemon, zested
½ tsp salt
½ tsp freshly ground black pepper
4 frozen filo dough, thawed
1 tbsp extra-virgin olive oil

DIRECTIONS

In a bowl, combine kale, artichoke, ricotta, parmesan, goat cheese, egg white, basil, lemon zest, salt, and pepper. Place a filo dough on a clean flat surface. Brush with olive oil.

Place a second filo sheet on the first and brush with more oil. Continue layering to form a pile of four oiled sheets. Working from the short side, cut the phyllo sheets into 8 strips and half them.

Spoon 1 tablespoon of filling onto one short end of every strip. Fold a corner to cover the filling and a triangle; continue folding over and over to the end of the strip, creating a triangle-shaped filo packet.

Repeat the process with the other filo bites. Place a trivet into the pot. Pour in 1 cup of water. Place the bites on top of the trivet. Seal the lid and cook on High Pressure for 15 minutes. Do a quick release.

Buttered Leeks with Poached Eggs

Servings: 3 | Prep + Cook Time: 15 minutes

INGREDIENTS

1 cup leeks, chopped into 1-inch pieces
6 eggs
2 tbsp oil
1 tbsp butter
1 tsp mustard seeds
1 tbsp dried rosemary
¼ tsp chili flakes
¼ tsp salt

DIRECTIONS

Heat oil on Sauté and add mustard seeds. Stir-fry for 2-3 minutes. Add leeks and butter. Cook for 5 minutes, stirring occasionally.

Crack eggs and season with dried rosemary, chili flakes, and salt. Cook until set, for about 4 minutes. Press Cancel and serve immediately.

Cheesy Broccoli & Bell Pepper Frittata

Servings: 4 | Prep + Cook Time: 30 minutes

INGREDIENTS

4 eggs
8 oz spinach, finely chopped
½ cup cheddar cheese
½ cup fresh ricotta cheese
3 cherry tomatoes, halved
¼ cup red bell pepper, chopped
1 cup chopped broccoli, pre-cooked
4 tbsp olive oil
½ tsp salt
¼ tsp freshly ground black pepper
¼ tsp dried oregano
½ cup fresh celery leaves, finely chopped

DIRECTIONS

Heat olive oil on Sauté. Add spinach and cook for 5 minutes, stirring occasionally. Add tomatoes, peppers, and broccoli. Cook for more 3-4 minutes.

In a bowl, Whisk 2 eggs, cheddar, and ricotta. Pour in the pot and cook for 2 more minutes. Then, crack the remaining 2 eggs and cook for another 5 minutes.

When done, press Cancel. Serve immediately with chopped celery leaves.

Funghi & Aglio Pizza

Servings: 2 | Prep + Cook Time: 25 minutes

INGREDIENTS

1 cup flour
½ tsp brown sugar
1 tsp garlic powder
2 tsp dried yeast
¼ tsp salt
1 tbsp olive oil

1 cup water
1 cup button mushrooms, chopped
¼ cup Gouda, grated
2 tbsp tomato paste, sugar-free
½ tsp dried oregano
¼ cup lukewarm water

DIRECTIONS

In a bowl fitted with a dough hook attachment, combine flour with brown sugar, dried yeast, and salt. Mix well and gradually add lukewarm water and oil. Continue to beat on high speed until smooth dough.

Transfer to a lightly floured surface and knead until completely smooth. Form into a tight ball and wrap tightly in plastic foil. Set aside for one hour. Line a baking dish with some parchment paper and set aside.

Roll out the dough with a rolling pin and transfer to the baking dish. Brush with tomato paste and sprinkle with oregano, gouda, and button mushrooms. Add a trivet inside your Instant Pot and pour in 1 cup of water. Put the dish on the trivet. Seal the lid, and cook for 15 minutes on High Pressure. Do a quick release. Remove the pizza from the pot using a parchment paper. Cut and serve.

Pizza Quattro Formaggi

Servings: 4 | Prep + Cook Time: 25 minutes

INGREDIENTS

1 pizza crust
½ cup tomato paste
¼ cup water
1 tsp dried oregano
1 oz cheddar cheese

5-6 slices mozzarella
¼ cup grated gouda
¼ cup grated parmesan
½ cup grated gouda cheese
2 tbsp extra virgin olive oil

DIRECTIONS

Grease the bottom of a baking dish with one tablespoon of olive oil. Line some parchment paper. Flour the working surface and roll out the pizza dough to the approximate size of your instant pot. Gently fit the dough in the previously prepared baking dish.

In a small bowl, combine tomato paste with water, and dry oregano. Spread the mixture over dough and finish with cheeses.

Add a trivet inside your the pot and pour in 1 cup of water. Seal the lid, and cook for 15 minutes on High Pressure. Do a quick release. Remove the pizza from the pot using a parchment paper. Cut and serve.

Feta Turkey Meatballs with Tomato Sauce

Servings: 6 | Prep + Cook Time: 50 minutes

INGREDIENTS

1 pound ground turkey
1 carrot, shredded
2 celery stalks, minced
¼ cup feta cheese, crumbled
¼ cup hot sauce
¼ cup bread crumbs

1 egg, beaten
2 tbsp olive oil
½ cup water
4 tomatoes, chopped
Salt and pepper to taste
2 tsp fresh parsley, chopped

DIRECTIONS

In a bowl, combine turkey, carrot, celery, feta cheese, hot sauce, breadcrumbs, and egg. Season with salt and pepper. Shape the mixture into 12 meatballs.

Heat oil on Sauté and fry the meatballs in batches until lightly golden. Pour in water, tomatoes, and salt. Seal the lid and cook on High Pressure for 5 minutes. Do a quick release. Sprinkle with parsley and serve.

Herbed Garlic Shrimp

Servings: 4 | Prep + Cook Time: 15 minutes

INGREDIENTS

1 pound shrimp, peeled and deveined
½ cup olive oil
1 tsp garlic powder
1 tsp dried rosemary, crushed

½ tsp dried basil
½ tsp dried sage
½ tsp salt
1 tsp chili pepper

DIRECTIONS

Pour 1 ½ cups of water in the inner pot. In a bowl, mix oil, garlic, rosemary, basil, sage, salt, and chili. Brush the marinade over shrimp.

Insert the steamer rack, and arrange the shrimp on top. Seal the lid and cook on Steam for 3 minutes on High. Release the steam naturally, for 10 minutes.

Press Sauté and stir-fry for 2 more minutes, or until golden brown.

Spinach Poached Egg Pancakes

Servings: 2 | Prep + Cook Time: 20 minutes

INGREDIENTS

6 oz spinach, chopped
2 eggs
3 tbsp oil
½ tsp garlic powder

¼ tsp dried oregano
¼ tsp dried rosemary
½ tsp sea salt
Kalamata olives and red bell peppers, for garnishing

DIRECTIONS

Heat the oil on Sauté and add chopped spinach. Season with salt and garlic powder. Give it a good stir and cook for 5 minutes, until soft.

Crack eggs and season with oregano, rosemary, and salt. Cook until completely set, for about 5 more minutes. Transfer to a serving plate and serve with kalamata olives or chopped red bell peppers.

Tasty Meatballs with Dilled Yogurt Dip

Servings: 4 | Prep + Cook Time: 35 minutes

INGREDIENTS

1 lb lean ground beef
2 garlic cloves, crushed
¼ cup flour
1 tbsp fresh rosemary, crushed
1 large egg, beaten
½ tsp salt
3 tbsp olive oil
1 cup Greek yogurt
2 tbsp fresh dill
1 garlic clove, crushed

DIRECTIONS

In a bowl, mix ground beef, garlic, rosemary, egg, and salt. Lightly dampen hands and shape balls. Grease the cooker with oil. Transfer the balls to the pot. Add 1 cup of water. Seal the lid and cook on High Pressure for 13 minutes. Do a quick release. For the dip, mix Greek yogurt, dill, and garlic. Stir well and drizzle over meatballs.

Green Onions Steamed Eggs

Serve: 1 | Prep + Cook Time: 10 minutes

INGREDIENTS

2 eggs
1 tbsp green onions, chopped
½ cup water
¼ tsp garlic powder
½ tsp salt
¼ tsp black pepper

DIRECTIONS

In a bowl, whisk eggs and water. Add the remaining ingredients and stir well. Transfer the mixture to a heat-proof bowl, that fits in your instant pot. Add 1 cup of water in the pot. Set the steamer tray and place the bowl on top. Seal the lid and cook on High Pressure for 5 minutes. Do a quick release.

Tangy Cheesy Arancini

Servings: 6 | Prep + Cook Time: 60 minutes

INGREDIENTS

½ cup olive oil, plus 1 tbsp
1 white onion, diced
2 garlic cloves, minced
5 cups chicken stock
½ cup apple cider vinegar
2 cups short grain rice
1½ cups grated Cheddar cheese,
¼ cup grated Parmesan cheese for garnish
1 cup canned kernel sweet corn, drained
1 tsp salt
1 tsp ground black pepper
2 cups fresh bread crumbs
2 eggs

DIRECTIONS

On Sauté, heat 1 tbsp of oil and sauté onion for 2 minutes until translucent. Add the garlic and cook for a minute. Stir in the stock and rice. Seal the lid and cook on High Pressure for 7 minutes. Do a natural pressure release for 10 minutes. Stir in cheddar cheese, corn, salt, and pepper. Spoon into a bowl and let cool. Wipe clean the pot.

In a bowl, pour the breadcrumbs. In a separate bowl, beat the eggs. Form balls out of the rice mixture, dip each into the beaten eggs, and coat in the breadcrumb mixture.

Heat the remaining oil on Sauté and fry in batches arancini until crispy and golden brown. Sprinkle with Parmesan cheese and serve.

SOUPS & SAUCES

Traditional Minestrone

Servings: 6 | Prep + Cook Time: 25 minutes

INGREDIENTS

2 tbsp olive oil
1 onion, diced
1 cup celery, chopped
1 carrot, peeled and diced
1 green bell pepper, chopped
2 cloves garlic, minced
3 cups chicken broth
½ tsp dried parsley
½ tsp dried thyme
½ tsp dried oregano

½ tsp salt
¼ tsp ground black pepper
2 bay leaves
28 ounces canned diced tomatoes
6 ounces canned tomato paste
2 cups kale
14 oz canned navy beans, rinsed and drained
½ cup white rice
¼ cup Parmesan cheese

DIRECTIONS

Warm olive oil on Sauté. Stir in carrot, celery and onion and cook for 5 to 6 minutes until soft. Add garlic and bell pepper and cook for 2 minutes as you stir until aromatic. Stir in pepper, thyme, stock, salt, parsley, oregano, tomatoes, bay leaves, and tomato paste to dissolve. Mix in rice.

Seal the lid and cook on High Pressure for 15 minutes. Do a quick release. Add kale to the liquid and stir. Use residual heat in slightly wilting the greens. Discard bay leaves. Stir in navy beans and serve topped with Parmesan cheese.

Cream of Mushroom & Spinach Soup

Servings: 4 | Prep + Cook Time: 25 minutes

INGREDIENTS

1 tbsp olive oil
8 Button Mushrooms, chopped
1 cup spinach, chopped
1 red onion, chopped
4 cups vegetable stock
2 sweet potatoes, peeled and chopped

2 tbsp white wine
1 tbsp dry Porcini mushrooms, soaked and drained
½ tsp sea salt
1 cup creme fraiche
½ tsp freshly ground black pepper

DIRECTIONS

Set on Sauté and add in olive oil and mushrooms. Sauté for 3 to 5 minutes until browning on both sides; Set aside. Add onion and spinach, and cook for 3 to 5 minutes until the onion becomes translucent.

Stir in chopped mushrooms, and cook for a further 5 minutes, stirring occasionally, until golden brown.

Pour in wine to deglaze the bottom of the pot, scrape to remove browned bits. Cook for 5 minutes until wine evaporates. Mix in the remaining mushrooms, potatoes, soaked mushrooms, wine, stock, and salt.

Seal the lid and cook on High Pressure for 5 minutes. Quick release the pressure. Add in pepper and creme fraiche to mix. Using an immersion blender, whizz the mixture until smooth. Stir in the sautéed mushrooms. Add reserved mushrooms for garnish before serving.

Andalusian Lentil Soup

Servings: 6 | Prep + Cook Time: 50 minutes

INGREDIENTS

2 ½ cups vegetable broth
1 ½ cups tomato sauce
1 onion, chopped
1 cup dry red lentils
½ cup prepared salsa verde
2 garlic cloves, minced

1 tbsp smoked paprika
2 tsp ground cumin
1 tsp chili powder
¼ tsp cayenne pepper
salt and ground black pepper to taste
Crushed tortilla chips for garnish

DIRECTIONS

Add in tomato sauce, broth, onion, salsa verde, cumin, cayenne pepper, chili powder, garlic, lentils, paprika, salt and pepper. Seal the lid and cook for 20 minutes on High Pressure.

Release pressure naturally, for 10 minutes. Divide into serving bowls and add crushed tortilla topping.

Bean & Zucchini Soup

Servings: 5 | Prep + Cook Time: 35 minutes

INGREDIENTS

1 tbsp olive oil
1 onion, chopped
2 cloves garlic, minced
5 cups vegetable broth
1 cup dried chickpeas
½ cup dried pinto beans, soaked overnight

½ cup dried navy beans, soaked overnight
3 carrots, chopped
1 large celery stalk, chopped
1 tsp dried thyme
16 oz zucchini noodles
Salt and black pepper, to taste

DIRECTIONS

Warm oil on Sauté. Stir in garlic and onion and cook for 5 minutes until golden brown. Mix in pepper, broth, carrots, salt, celery, beans, and thyme.

Seal the lid and cook for 15 minutes on High Pressure. Release the pressure naturally for 10 minutes.

Mix zucchini noodles into the soup and stir until wilted. Taste and adjust the seasoning.

Jalapeño Green Sauce

Servings: 4 | Prep + Cook Time: 8 minutes

INGREDIENTS

4 oz green jalapeno peppers, chopped
1 green bell pepper, chopped
2 garlic cloves, crushed
½ cup white vinegar

1 tbsp apple cider vinegar
1 tsp sea salt
4 tbsp water

DIRECTIONS

Add all ingredients to the instant pot. Seal the lid and cook on High Pressure for 2 minutes. When done, release the steam naturally, for about 5 minutes.

Transfer to a blender, pulse until combined and store in jars.

Tip: Strain the mixture if you prefer more liquid sauce.

Parsley Garden Vegetable Soup

Servings: 8 | Prep + Cook Time: 42 minutes

INGREDIENTS

2 tbsp olive oil
1 cup leeks, chopped
2 garlic cloves, minced
8 cups vegetable stock
1 carrot, diced
1 potato, diced
1 celery stalk, diced
1 cup mushrooms
1 cup broccoli florets
1 cup cauliflower florets
½ red bell pepper, diced
¼ head green cabbage, chopped
½ cup green beans
½ salt, or more to taste
½ tsp ground black pepper
½ cup fresh parsley, chopped

DIRECTIONS

Heat oil on Sauté. Add in garlic and onion and cook for 6 minutes until slightly browned. Add in stock, carrot, celery, broccoli, bell pepper, green beans, salt, cabbage, cauliflower, mushrooms, potato, and pepper.

Seal lid; cook on High for 6 minutes. Release pressure naturally for about 5 minutes. Stir in parsley and serve.

Chorizo Sausage & Fire-Roasted Tomato Soup

Servings: 6 | Prep + Cook Time: 30 minutes

INGREDIENTS

1 tbsp olive oil
2 shallots, chopped
3 cloves garlic, minced
1 tsp salt
4 cups beef broth
28 oz fire-roasted diced tomatoes
½ cup fresh ripe tomatoes
1 tbsp red wine vinegar
3 chorizo sausage, chopped
½ tsp ground black pepper
½ cup thinly chopped fresh basil

DIRECTIONS

Warn oil on Sauté and cook chorizo until crispy. Remove to a to a plate lined with paper towel.

Add in garlic and onion and cook for 5 minutes until soft. Season with salt. Stir in red wine vinegar, broth, diced tomatoes, sun-dried tomatoes, and black pepper into the cooker.

Seal the lid and cook on High Pressure for 8 minutes. Release the ´pressure quickly. Pour the soup into a blender and process until smooth. Divide into bowls, top with chorizo and decorate with basil.

Lamb & Spinach Soup

Servings: 5 | Prep + Cook Time: 50 minutes

INGREDIENTS

1 lb of lamb shoulder, cut into bite-sized pieces
10 oz fresh spinach leaves, chopped
3 eggs, beaten
5 cups vegetable broth
3 tbsp olive oil
1 tsp salt

DIRECTIONS

Place in your instant pot the lamb along with the remaining ingredients. Seal the lid, press Soup/Broth and cook for 30 minutes on High Pressure. Do a natural pressure release, for about 10 minutes.

Turkish Leek & Potato Soup

Servings: 5 | Prep + Cook Time: 30 minutes

INGREDIENTS

2 tbsp butter
3 leeks, white part only, chopped
2 cloves garlic, minced
4 cups vegetable broth
3 potatoes, peeled and cubed

½ cup sour cream
2 tbsp rosemary
2 bay leaves
salt and ground black pepper to taste
2 tbsp fresh chives, to garnish

DIRECTIONS

Melt butter on Sauté mode. Stir in garlic and leeks and cook for 3 to 4 minutes, until soft. Stir in bay leaves, potatoes, and broth. Seal the lid and cook on High Pressure for 15 minutes. Release pressure quickly. Remove the bay leaves and cobs and discard.

Transfer soup to immersion blender and puree soup to obtain a smooth consistency. Season with salt and pepper. Top with diced chives and sour cream.

Classic Bolognese Sauce

Servings: 8 | Prep + Cook Time: 45 minutes

INGREDIENTS

4 slices bacon, chopped
1 tbsp olive oil
1 onion, minced
2 celery stalks, minced
1 carrot, chopped
1½ pounds ground beef

3 tbsp red wine
28 ounces italian canned tomatoes, crushed
2 bay leaves
Salt and pepper to taste
½ cup yogurt
¼ cup chopped fresh basil

DIRECTIONS

Set on Sauté, and cook bacon until crispy, for 4 to 5 minutes. Mix in celery, butter, carrots, and onion, and continue cooking for about 5 minutes until vegetables are softened.

Mix in ¼ teaspoon pepper, ½ teaspoon salt, and beef, and cook for 4 minutes until golden brown. Stir in the wine and allow to soak, approximately 4 more minutes.

Add in bay leaves, tomatoes, and remaining pepper and salt. Seal the lid and cook for 15 minutes on High. Release Pressure naturally for 10 minutes. Add yogurt and stir. Serve with noodles and use basil to garnish.

Power Green Soup

Servings: 3 | Prep + Cook Time: 35 minutes

INGREDIENTS

1 lb fresh brussels sprouts, rinsed, halved, chopped
6 oz fresh baby spinach, rinsed, torn, chopped
1 tsp sea salt
1 tbsp whole milk

3 tbsp sour cream
1 tbsp fresh celery, chopped
3 cups water
1 tbsp butter

DIRECTIONS

Add all ingredients to the instant pot. Seal the lid and set the steam release. Press Soup/Broth and cook for 30 minutes on High. Do a quick release. Transfer to a food processor. and blend well to combine.

Italian Broccoli & Potato Soup

Servings: 4 | Prep + Cook Time: 45 minutes

INGREDIENTS

1 lb broccoli, cut into florets
2 potatoes, peeled, chopped
4 cups vegetable broth
½ tsp dried rosemary
½ tsp salt
½ cup sour cream

DIRECTIONS

Place broccoli and potatoes in the pot. Pour the broth and seal the lid. Cook on Soup/Broth for 20 minutes on High. Do a quick release and remove to a blender. Pulse to combine. Stir in sour cream and add salt.

Spanish Fall Soup

Servings: 4 | Prep + Cook Time: 34 minutes

INGREDIENTS

3 sweet potatoes, chopped
1 tsp sea salt
2 fennel bulb, chopped
16 oz pureed pumpkin
1 large onion, chopped
1 tbsp coconut oil
4 cups water
1 tbsp sour cream

DIRECTIONS

Heat the oil on Sauté, and add onion and fennel bulb. Cook for 3-5 minutes, until tender and translucent. Add the remaining ingredients and seal the lid. Cook on High pressure for 25 minutes. Do a quick release, transfer the soup to a blender and blend for 20 seconds until creamy. Top with sour cream and serve.

Broccoli Soup with Gorgonzola

Servings: 4 | Prep + Cook Time: 35 minutes

INGREDIENTS

8 oz Gorgonzola cheese, crumbled
1 cup broccoli, finely chopped
4 cups water
1 tbsp olive oil
½ cup full-fat milk
1 tbsp parsley, finely chopped
½ tsp salt
¼ tsp black pepper, ground

DIRECTIONS

Add all ingredients to the pot, seal the lid and cook on Soup/Broth mode for 30 minutes on High Pressure. Do a quick release. Remove the lid and sprinkle with fresh parsley. Serve warm.

Maltese Chickpea & Carrot Soup

Servings: 6 | Prep + Cook Time: 15 minutes

INGREDIENTS

14 oz chickpeas, soaked, rinsed, drained
2 carrots, chopped
2 onions, peeled, chopped
2 tomatoes, peeled, chopped
3 tbsp tomato paste
A handful of fresh chopped parsley
2 cups vegetable broth
2 tbsp olive oil
1 tsp salt

DIRECTIONS

To the instant Pot, add chickpeas, oil, onions, carrot, and tomatoes. Pour in the broth and sprinkle salt. Stir in the paste and seal the lid. Cook on High Pressure for 6 minutes. Do a quick release. Sprinkle with parsley, to serve.

Creamy Asparagus Soup

Servings: 4 | Prep + Cook Time: 40 minutes

INGREDIENTS

2 lb fresh asparagus, trimmed, 1-inch thick
2 onions, peeled and finely chopped
1 cup heavy cream
4 cups vegetable broth
2 tbsp butter
1 tbsp vegetable oil
½ tsp salt
½ tsp dried oregano
½ tsp paprika

DIRECTIONS

Warm butter and oil on Sauté. Stir-fry the onions for 2 minutes, until translucent. Add asparagus, oregano, salt, and paprika. Stir well and cook until asparagus soften, for a few minutes. Pour in the broth. Seal the lid and cook on Soup/Broth for 20 minutes on High. Do a quick release and whisk in the heavy cream. Serve chilled or warm.

Old-Fashioned Chicken Soup

Servings: 4 | Prep + Cook Time: 40 minutes

INGREDIENTS

1 lb chicken breast, boneless, skinless, chopped
1 onion, chopped
1 carrot, chopped
2 small potatoes, peeled, chopped
1 tsp cayenne pepper
2 egg yolks
1 tsp salt
3 tbsp lemon juice
3 tbsp olive oil
4 cups water

DIRECTIONS

Add all ingredients to the pot, and seal the lid. Set the steam release handle and cook on Soup/Broth mode for 20 minutes on High. Release the pressure naturally, for 10 minutes, open the lid and serve.

White Bean Pomodoro Soup

Servings: 4 | Prep + Cook Time: 40 minutes

INGREDIENTS

2 lb tomatoes, diced
1 cup white beans, pre-cooked
1 small onion, diced
2 garlic cloves, crushed
1 cup heavy cream
1 cup vegetable broth
2 tbsp fresh parsley, finely chopped
¼ tsp black pepper, ground
2 tbsp extra virgin olive oil
½ tsp salt

DIRECTIONS

Warm oil on Sauté mode. Stir-fry onion and garlic on Sauté, for 2 minutes. Add tomatoes, beans, broth, 3 cups of water, parsley, salt, pepper, and a little bit of sugar to balance the bitterness. Seal the lid and cook on Soup/Broth for 30 minutes on High Pressure. Release the pressure naturally, for 10 minutes. Top with a dollop of sour cream and chopped parsley, to serve.

Feta-Topped Potato Gazpacho

Servings: 4 | Prep + Cook Time: 25 minutes

INGREDIENTS

3 large leeks
3 tbsp butter
1 onion, thinly chopped
1 lb potatoes, chopped
5 cups vegetable stock
2 tsp lemon juice
¼ tsp nutmeg
¼ tsp ground coriander
1 bay leaf
5 oz feta, crumbled
Salt and white pepper
Freshly snipped chives, to garnish

DIRECTIONS

Remove most of the green parts of the leeks. Slice the white parts very finely. Melt butter on Sauté, and stir-fry leeks and onion for 5 minutes without browning. Add potatoes, stock, juice, nutmeg, coriander and bay leaf. Season to taste with salt and pepper, and seal the lid.

Press Manual/Pressure Cook and set the timer to 10 minutes. Cook on High Pressure. Do a quick release and discard the bay leaf. Process the soup in a food processor until smooth. Season to taste, add feta. Serve the soup sprinkled with freshly snipped chives.

Classic Napoli Sauce

Servings: 4 | Prep + Cook Time: 45 minutes

INGREDIENTS

1 lb mushrooms
2 cups canned tomatoes, diced
1 carrot, chopped
1 onion, chopped
1 celery stick, chopped
1 tbsp olive oil
1 tsp salt
½ tsp paprika
1 tsp fish sauce
1 cup water

DIRECTIONS

Heat olive oil on Sauté. Stir-fry carrot, onion, celery, and paprika, for 5 minutes. Add all remaining ingredients, except for the tomatoes, and cook for 5-6 more minutes, until the meat is slightly browned. Seal the lid.

Cook on High Pressure for 20 minutes. When done, release the steam naturally, for about 10 minutes. Hit Sauté, and cook for 7-8 minutes, to thicken the sauce.

Effortless Chicken Rice Soup

Servings: 4 | Prep + Cook Time: 20 minutes

INGREDIENTS

1 lb chicken breast, boneless, skinless, cut into pieces
1 large carrot, chopped
1 onion, chopped
¼ cup rice
1 potato, finely chopped
½ tsp salt
1 tsp cayenne pepper
A handful of parsley, finely chopped
3 tbsp olive oil
4 cups chicken broth

DIRECTIONS

Add all ingredients, except parsley, to the pot, and seal the lid. Cook on Soup/Broth for 15 minutes on High. Do a quick pressure release. Stir in fresh parsley and serve.

GRAINS & PASTA

Spanish Chorizo & Spicy Lentils Stew

Servings: 10 | Prep + Cook Time: 50 minutes

INGREDIENTS

2 cups lentils, drained and rinsed
7 ounces Spanish chorizo, chopped
1 onion, diced
2 garlic cloves, crushed
2 cups tomato sauce
2 cups vegetable broth
½ cup mustard
½ cup cider vinegar
3 tbsp Worcestershire sauce

2 tbsp maple syrup
2 tbsp liquid smoke
1 tbsp lime juice
2 cups brown sugar
1 tbsp salt
1 tbsp ground black pepper
1 tsp chili powder
1 tsp paprika
¼ tsp cayenne pepper

DIRECTIONS

Set on Sauté mode, add in chorizo and cook for 3 minutes as you stir until crisp. Add garlic and onion and cook for 2 minutes until translucent. Mix tomato sauce, broth, cider vinegar, liquid smoke, Worcestershire sauce, lime juice, mustard, and maple syrup in a mixing bowl.

Pour the mixture in the Pressure cooker to deglaze the pan, scrape the bottom of the pan to do away with any browned bits of food. Add pepper, chili, sugar, paprika, salt, and cayenne into the sauce mixture as you stir to mix.

Stir in lentils to coat. Seal the lid and cook on High Pressure for 30 minutes.

Release pressure naturally for 10 minutes.

Moroccan Chicken & Chickpea Stew

Servings: 6 | Prep + Cook Time: 40 minutes

INGREDIENTS

1 pound boneless, skinless chicken legs
2 tspg round cumin
½ tsp cayenne pepper
2 tbsp olive oil
1 onion, minced
2 jalapeño peppers, deseeded and minced
3 garlic cloves, crushed
2 tsp freshly grated ginger

¼ cup chicken stock
1 (24 ounces) can crushed tomatoes
2 (14 ounces) cans chickpeas, drained and rinsed
Salt to taste
½ cup coconut milk
¼ cup fresh parsley, chopped
2 cups hot cooked basmati rice

DIRECTIONS

Season the chicken with 1 tsp salt, cayenne pepper, and cumin. Set on Sauté and warm the oil. Add in jalapeño peppers, and onion, and cook for 5 minutes. Mix in ginger and garlic, and cook for 3 minutes until tender.

Add ¼ cup chicken stock into the cooker to ensure the pan is deglazed, from the pan's bottom scrape any browned bits of food. Mix the onion mixture with chickpeas, tomatoes, and salt. Stir in Seasoned chicken to coat in sauce.

Seal the lid and cook on High Pressure for 20 minutes. Release the pressure quickly. Remove the chicken and slice into chunks. Into the remaining sauce, mix in coconut milk; simmer for 5 minutes on Keep Warm. Split rice into 4 bowls. Top with chicken, then sauce and add cilantro for garnish.

Asparagus & Shrimp Risotto

Servings: 4 | Prep + Cook Time: 1 hour 15 minutes

INGREDIENTS

1 tbsp olive oil
1 pound asparagus, trimmed and roughly chopped
1 cup spinach, chopped
1½ cups mushrooms, chopped
1 cup rice, rinsed and drained
1¼ cups chicken broth

¾ cup milk
1 tbsp coconut oil
16 shrimp, cleaned and deveined
Salt and ground black pepper to taste
¾ cup Parmesan cheese, shredded

DIRECTIONS

Warm the oil on Sauté. Add spinach, mushrooms and asparagus and Sauté for 10 minutes until cooked through. Press Cancel. Add rice, milk and chicken broth to the pot as you stir.

Seal the lid, press Multigrain and cook for 40 minutes on High Pressure. Do a quick release, open the lid and put the rice on a serving plate.

Take back the empty pot to the pressure cooker, add coconut oil and press Sauté. Add shrimp and cook each side taking 4 minutes until cooked through and turns pink. Set shrimp over rice, add pepper and salt for seasoning. Serve topped with shredded Parmesan cheese.

Garbanzo Beans with Pancetta

Servings: 6 | Prep + Cook Time: 50 minutes

INGREDIENTS

3 strips pancetta
1 onion, diced
15 oz canned garbanzo beans
2 cups water
1 cup apple cider
2 garlic cloves, minced

½ cup ketchup
¼ cup sugar
1 tsp ground mustard powder
1 tsp salt
1 tsp black pepper
Fresh parsley to garnish

DIRECTIONS

Cook pancetta for 5 minutes, until crispy, on Sauté mode. Add onion and garlic, and cook for 3 minutes until soft. Mix in garbanzo beans, ketchup, sugar, salt, apple cider, mustard powder, water, and pepper.

Seal the lid, press Bean/Chili and cook on High Pressure for 30 minutes. Release Pressure naturally for 10 minutes. Serve in bowls garnished with parsley.

Rice & Olives Stuffed Mushrooms

Servings: 4 | Prep + Cook Time: 45 minutes

INGREDIENTS

4 large portobello mushrooms, stems and gills removed
2 tbsp melted butter
½ cup brown rice, cooked
1 tomato, seed removed and chopped
¼ cup black olives, pitted and chopped
1 green bell pepper, seeded and diced

½ cup feta cheese, crumbled
Juice of 1 lemon
½ tsp salt
½ tsp ground black pepper
Minced fresh cilantro, for garnish
1 cup vegetable broth

DIRECTIONS

Brush the mushrooms with butter. Arrange the mushrooms in a single layer in an oiled baking pan. In a bowl, mix the rice, tomato, olives, bell pepper, feta cheese, lemon juice, salt, and black pepper.

Spoon the rice mixture into the mushrooms. Pour in the broth, seal the lid and cook on High Pressure for 10 minutes. Do a quick release. Garnish with fresh cilantro and serve immediately.

Pasta Shells Filled with Ricotta & Spinach

Servings: 6 | Prep + Cook Time: 1 hour

INGREDIENTS

2 cups onion, chopped
1 cup carrot, chopped
3 garlic cloves, minced
3 ½ tbsp olive oil,
1 (28 ounces) canned tomatoes, crushed
12 ounces conchiglie pasta
1 tbsp olive oil
2 cups ricotta cheese, crumbled

1 ½ cup feta cheese, crumbled
2 cups spinach, chopped
¾ cup grated Pecorino Romano cheese
2 tbsp chopped fresh chives
1 tbsp chopped fresh dill
Salt and ground black pepper to taste
1 cup shredded cheddar cheese

DIRECTIONS

Warm olive oil on Sauté. Add in onion, carrot, and garlic, and cook for 5 minutes until tender. Stir in tomatoes and cook for another 10 minutes. Remove to a bowl and set aside.

Wipe the pot with a damp cloth, add pasta and cover with enough water. Seal the lid and cook for 5 minutes on High Pressure. Do a quick release and drain the pasta. Lightly Grease olive oil to a baking sheet.

In a bowl, combine feta and ricotta cheese. Add in spinach, Pecorino Romano cheese, dill, and chives, and stir well. Adjust the seasonings. Using a spoon, fill the shells with the mixture.

Spread 4 cups tomato sauce on the baking sheet. Place the stuffed shells over with seam-sides down and sprinkle cheddar cheese atop. Use aluminum foil to the cover the baking dish.

Pour 1 cup of water in the pot of the Pressure cooker and insert the trivet. Lower the baking dish onto the trivet. Seal the lid, and cook for 15 minutes on High Pressure. Do a quick release. Take away the foil. Place the stuffed shells to serving plates and top with tomato sauce before serving.

Chili-Garlic Rice with Halloumi

Servings: 6 | Prep + Cook Time: 20 minutes

INGREDIENTS

2 cups water
2 tbsp brown sugar
2 tbsp rice vinegar
1 tbsp sweet chili sauce
1 tbsp olive oil

1 tsp fresh minced garlic
20 ounces Halloumi cheese, cubed
1 cup rice
¼ cup chopped fresh chives, for garnish

DIRECTIONS

Heat the oil on Sauté and fry the halloumi for 5 minutes until golden brown. Set aside.

To the pot, add water, garlic, olive oil, vinegar, sugar, soy sauce, and chili sauce and mix well until smooth. Stir in rice noodles. Seal the lid and cook on High Pressure for 3 minutes. Release the Pressure quickly. Split the rice between bowls. Top with fried halloumi and sprinkle with fresh chives before serving.

Cannellini Bean Stew with Spinach

Servings: 4 | Prep + Cook Time: 45 minutes

INGREDIENTS

2 tbsp olive oil
1 onion, chopped
2 cloves garlic, minced
2 carrots, peeled and chopped
1 cup celery, chopped
4 cups vegetable broth

1 cup cannellini beans, soaked, drained, rinsed
1 tsp dried thyme
1 tsp dried rosemary
1 bay leaf
1 cup spinach, torn into pieces
Salt and black pepper to taste

DIRECTIONS

Warm olive oil on Sauté. Stir in garlic and onion, and cook for 3 minutes until tender and fragrant. Mix in celery and carrots and cook for 2 to 3 minutes more until they start to soften. Add broth, bay leaf, thyme, rosemary, cannellini beans, and salt.

Seal the lid and cook for 30 minutes on High Pressure. Quick release the pressure and stir in spinach. Allow to sit for 2 to 4 minutes until the spinach wilts, and season with pepper and salt.

Creamy Grana Padano Risotto

Servings: 6 | Prep + Cook Time: 25 minutes

INGREDIENTS

1 tbsp olive oil
1 white onion, chopped
1 tbsp butter
2 cups Carnaroli rice, rinsed
¼ cup dry white wine

4 cups chicken stock
1 tsp salt
½ tsp ground white pepper
2 tbsp Grana padano cheese, grated
¼ tbsp Grana padano cheese, flakes

DIRECTIONS

Warm oil on Sauté. Stir-fry onion for 3 minutes until soft and translucent. Add in butter and rice and cook for 5 minutes stirring occasionally.

Pour wine into the pot to deglaze, scrape away any browned bits of food from the pan.

Stir in stock, pepper, and salt to the pot. Seal the lid, press Rice and cook on High for 15 minutes. Release the Pressure quickly.

Sprinkle with grated Parmesan cheese and stir well. Top with flaked cheese for garnish before serving.

Rigatoni with Sausage and Spinach

Servings: 4 | Prep + Cook Time: 30 minutes

INGREDIENTS

1 tbsp butter
½ cup diced red bell pepper
1 onion, chopped
3 cups vegetable broth
¼ cup tomato purée
4 sausage links, chopped

½ cup milk
2 tsp chili powder
Salt and ground black pepper to taste
12 ounces rigatoni pasta
1 cup baby spinach
½ cup Parmesan Cheese

DIRECTIONS

Warm butter on Sauté. Add red bell pepper, onion, and sausage, and cook for 5 minutes. Mix in broth, chili, tomato paste, salt, and pepper. Stir in rigatoni pasta.

Seal the lid and cook on High Pressure for 12 minutes. Naturally release Pressure for 10 minutes. Stir in spinach and let simmer until wilted. Sprinkle with Parmesan and serve.

Turkey Tortiglioni

Servings: 6 | Prep + Cook Time: 35 minutes

INGREDIENTS

2 tsp chili powder
1 tsp salt
1 tsp cumin
1 tsp onion powder
1 tsp garlic powder
½ tsp thyme
1 ½ pounds turkey breast, cut into strips
1 tbsp olive oil
1 red onion, cut into wedges
4 garlic cloves, minced

3 cups chicken broth
1 cup salsa
16 ounces tortiglioni
1 red bell pepper, chopped diagonally
1 yellow bell pepper, chopped diagonally
1 green bell pepper, chopped diagonally
1 cup shredded Gouda cheese
½ cup sour cream
½ cup chopped parsley

DIRECTIONS

In a bowl, mix chili powder, cumin, garlic powder, onion powder, salt, and oregano. Reserve 1 tsp of seasoning. Coat turkey with the remaining seasoning.

Warm oil on Sauté. Add in turkey strips and sauté for 4 to 5 minutes until browned. Place the turkey in a bowl. Sauté the onion and garlic for 1 minute in the cooker until soft. Press Cancel.

Mix in salsa, broth, and scrape the bottom of any brown bits. Into the broth mixture, stir in tortiglioni pasta and cover with bell peppers and chicken.

Seal the lid and cook for 5 minutes on High Pressure. Do a quick Pressure release.

Open the lid and sprinkle with shredded gouda cheese and reserved seasoning, and stir well. Divide into plates and top with sour cream. Add parsley for garnishing and serve.

Risoni with Carrots & Onion

Servings: 6 | Prep + Cook Time: 15 minutes

INGREDIENTS

1 cup orzo, rinsed
2 cups water
2 carrots, cut into sticks
1 large onion, chopped

2 tbsp olive oil
Salt to taste
Fresh cilantro, chopped for garnish

DIRECTIONS

Heat oil on Sauté. Add in onion and carrots and stir-fry for about 10 minutes until tender and crispy. Remove to a plate and set aside. Add water, salt and orzo in the instant pot.

Seal the lid and cook on High Pressure for 1 minute. Do a quick release. Fluff the cooked orzo with a fork. Transfer to a serving plate and top with the carrots and onion. Serve scattered with cilantro.

Crispy Feta with Roasted Butternut Squash & Rice

Servings: 4 | Prep + Cook Time: 30 minutes

INGREDIENTS

½ cup water
2 cups vegetable broth
1 small butternut squash, peeled and sliced
2 tablespoons melted butter, Divided
1 tsp salt

1 tsp freshly ground black pepper
1 cup feta cheese, cubed
1 tbsp coconut aminos
2 tsp arrowroot starch
1 cup jasmine rice, cooked

DIRECTIONS

Pour the rice and broth in the pot and stir to combine. In a bowl, toss butternut squash with 1 tbsp of melted butter and season with salt and black pepper.

In another bowl, mix the remaining butter, water and coconut aminos. Toss feta in the mixture, add the arrowroot starch, and toss again to combine well. Transfer to a greased baking dish.

Lay a trivet over the rice and place the baking dish on the trivet. Seal the lid and cook on High for 15 minutes. Do a quick pressure release. Fluff the rice with a fork and serve with squash and feta.

Veggie Arborio Rice Bowls with Pesto

Servings: 2 | Prep + Cook Time: 30 minutes

INGREDIENTS

1 cup arborio rice, rinsed and drained
2 cups vegetable broth
Salt and black pepper to taste
1 potato, peeled, cubed
1 head broccoli, cut into small florets

1 bunch baby carrots, peeled
¼ cabbage, chopped
2 eggs
¼ cup pesto sauce
Lemon wedges, for serving

DIRECTIONS

In the pot, mix broth, pepper, rice and salt. Set trivet to the inner pot on top of rice and add a steamer basket to the top of the trivet. Mix carrots, potato, eggs and broccoli in the steamer basket. Add pepper and salt for seasoning.

Seal the lid and cook for 1 minute on High Pressure. Quick-release the pressure.

Take away the trivet and steamer basket from the pot. Set the eggs in a bowl of ice water. Then peel and halve the eggs. Use a fork to fluff rice. Adjust the seasonings.

In two bowls, equally divide rice, broccoli, eggs, carrots, sweet potatoes, and a dollop of pesto. Serve alongside a lemon wedge.

Simple Carnaroli Rice

Servings: 4 | Prep + Cook Time: 25 minutes

INGREDIENTS

2 cups carnaroli rice
3 ½ cups water

salt and black pepper to taste

DIRECTIONS

Stir rice and water together in the cooker. Season with Salt to taste. Seal the lid and cook for 15 minutes on High Pressure. Release Pressure naturally for 10 minutes. Use a fork to fluff rice. Add black pepper before serving.

Rice Stuffing Zucchini Boats

Servings: 4 | Prep + Cook Time: 20 minutes

INGREDIENTS

2 small zucchini, halved lengthwise
½ cup cooked rice
½ cup canned white beans, drained and rinsed
½ cup chopped tomatoes
½ cup chopped toasted cashew nuts

½ cup grated Parmesan cheese
2 tbsp melted butter
½ tsp salt
½ tsp freshly ground black pepper

DIRECTIONS

Pour 1 cup of water in the instant pot and insert a trivet. Scoop out the pulp of zucchini and chop roughly.

In a bowl, mix the zucchini pulp, rice, tomatoes, cashew nuts, ¼ cup of Parmesan, 1 tbsp of melted butter, salt, and black pepper. Fill the zucchini boats with the mixture, and arrange the stuffed boats in a single layer on the trivet. Seal the lid and cook for 15 minutes on Steam on High. Do a quick release and serve.

Easy Spanish Rice

Servings: 4 | Prep + Cook Time: 30 minutes

INGREDIENTS

3 tbsp olive oil
1 small onion, chopped
2 garlic cloves, minced
1 serrano pepper, seeded and chopped
1 cup bomba rice

⅓ cup chunky salsa
¼ cup tomato sauce
½ cup vegetable broth
1 tsp salt
1 tbsp chopped fresh parsley

DIRECTIONS

Warm oil on Sauté and cook onion, garlic, and serrano pepper for 2 minutes, stirring occasionally until fragrant. Stir in rice, salsa, tomato sauce, vegetable broth, and salt.

Seal the lid and cook on High Pressure for 10 minutes. Do a natural pressure release for 10 minutes. Sprinkle with fresh parsley and serve.

Chard & Mushroom Risotto with Pumpkin Seeds

Servings: 4 | Prep + Cook Time: 30 minutes

INGREDIENTS

3 tbsp olive oil
1 onion, chopped
2 swiss chard, stemmed and chopped
1 cup risotto rice
⅓ cup white wine

3 cups vegetable stock
½ tsp salt
½ cup mushrooms
4 tbsp pumpkin seeds, toasted
⅓ cup grated Pecorino Romano cheese

DIRECTIONS

Heat oil on Sauté, and cook onion and mushrooms for 5 minutes, stirring, until tender. Add the rice and cook for a minute. Stir in wine and cook for 2 to 3 minutes until almost evaporated.

Pour in stock and season with salt. Seal the lid and cook on High Pressure for 10 minutes. Do a quick release. Stir in chard until wilted, mix in cheese to melt, and serve scattered with pumpkin seeds.

Cherry Tomato-Basil Linguine

Servings: 4 | Prep + Cook Time: 22 minutes

INGREDIENTS

2 tbsp olive oil
1 small onion, diced
2 garlic cloves, minced
1 cup cherry tomatoes, halved
1 ½ cups vegetable stock
¼ cup julienned basil leaves
1 tsp salt
½ tsp ground black pepper
¼ tsp red chili flakes
1 pound Linguine noodles, halved
Fresh basil leaves for garnish
1/2 cup Parmigiano-Reggiano cheese, grated

DIRECTIONS

Warm oil on Sauté. Add onion and Sauté for 2 minutes until soft. Mix garlic and tomatoes and sauté for 4 minutes. To the pot, add vegetable stock, salt, julienned basil, red chili flakes and pepper.

Add linguine to the tomato mixture until covered. Seal the lid and cook on High Pressure for 5 minutes.

Naturally release the pressure for 5 minutes. Stir the mixture to ensure it is broken down.

Divide into plates. Top with basil and Parmigiano-Reggiano cheese and serve.

Beef-Stuffed Pasta Shells

Servings: 4 | Prep + Cook Time: 35 minutes

INGREDIENTS

2 tbsp olive oil
1 pound ground beef
16 ounces pasta shells
2 cups water
15 ounces tomato sauce
15-ounce can black beans, drained and rinsed
15-ounces canned corn, drained (or 2 cups frozen corn)
10 ounces red enchilada sauce
4 ounces diced green chiles
1 cup shredded mozzarella cheese
Salt and ground black pepper to taste
Additional cheese for topping
Finely chopped parsley for garnish

DIRECTIONS

Heat oil on Sauté. Add ground beef and cook for 7 minutes until it starts to brown.

Mix in pasta, tomato sauce, enchilada sauce, black beans, water, corn, and green chiles and stir to coat well. Add more water if desired.

Seal the lid and cook on High Pressure for 10 minutes. Do a quick Pressure release. Into the pasta mixture, mix in mozzarella cheese until melted; add black pepper and salt. Garnish with parsley to serve.

Pasta Caprese Ricotta-Basil Fusilli

Servings: 3 | Prep + Cook Time: 15 minutes

INGREDIENTS

1 tbsp olive oil
1 onion, thinly chopped
6 garlic cloves, minced
1 tsp red pepper flakes
2 ½ cups dried fusilli
1 (15 ounces) can tomato sauce
1 cup tomatoes, halved
1 cup water
¼ cup basil leaves
1 tsp salt
1 cup Ricotta cheese, crumbled
2 tbsp chopped fresh basil

DIRECTIONS

Warm oil on Sauté. Add in red pepper flakes, garlic and onion and cook for 3 minutes until soft.

Mix in fusilli, tomatoes, half of the basil leaves, water, tomato sauce, and salt. Seal the lid, and cook on High Pressure for 4 minutes. Release the pressure quickly.

Transfer the pasta to a serving platter and top with the crumbled ricotta and remaining chopped basil.

Chicken Ragù Bolognese

Servings: 8 | Prep + Cook Time: 50 minutes

INGREDIENTS

2 tbsp olive oil
6 ounces bacon, cubed
1 onion, minced
1 carrot, minced
1 celery stalk, minced
2 garlic cloves, crushed
¼ cup tomato paste
¼ tsp crushed red pepper flakes
1 ½ pounds ground chicken
½ cup white wine
1 cup milk
1 cup chicken broth
Salt to taste
1 pound spaghetti

DIRECTIONS

Warm oil on Sauté. Add in bacon and fry for 5 minutes until crispy.

Add celery, carrot, garlic and onion and cook for 5 minutes until fragrant. Mix in red pepper flakes and tomato paste, and cook for 2 minutes. Break chicken into small pieces and place in the pot.

Cook for 10 minutes, as you stir, until browned. Pour in wine and simmer for 2 minutes. Add in chicken broth and milk. Seal the lid and cook for 15 minutes on High Pressure. Release the pressure quickly.

Add in the spaghetti and stir. Seal the lid, and cook on High Pressure for another 5 minutes.

Release the Pressure quickly. Check the pasta for doneness. Taste, adjust the seasoning and serve hot.

Squash Parmesan & Linguine

Servings: 4 | Prep + Cook Time: 45 minutes

INGREDIENTS

1 cup flour
2 tsp salt
2 eggs
4 cups water
1 cup seasoned breadcrumbs
½ cup grated Parmesan cheese, plus more for garnish
1 yellow squash, peeled and sliced
1 pound linguine
24 ounces canned Seasoned tomato sauce
2 tbsp olive oil
1 cup shredded mozzarella cheese
Minced fresh basil, for garnish

DIRECTIONS

Break the linguine in half. Put it in the pot and add water and half of salt. Seal the lid and cook on High Pressure for 5 minutes. Combine the flour and 1 teaspoon of salt in a bowl. In another bowl, whisk the eggs and 2 tbsp of water. In a third bowl, mix the breadcrumbs and mozzarella cheese.

Coat each squash slices in the flour. Shake off excess flour, dip in the egg wash, and dredge in the bread crumbs. Set aside. Quickly release the pressure. Remove linguine to a serving bowl and mix in the tomato sauce and sprinkle with fresh basil. Heat oil on Sauté and fry breaded squash until crispy.

Serve the squash topped mozzarella cheese with the linguine on side.

Pork Spaghetti with Spinach and Tomatoes

Servings: 4 | Prep + Cook Time: 35 minutes

INGREDIENTS

2 tbsp olive oil
½ cup onion, chopped
1 garlic clove, minced
1 pound pork sausage meat
2 cups water
1 (14 ounces) can diced tomatoes, drained
½ cup sun-dried tomatoes

1 tbsp dried oregano
1 teaspoon Italian seasoning
1 fresh jalapeño chile, stemmed, seeded, and minced
1 tsp salt
8 ounces dried spaghetti, halved
1 cup spinach

DIRECTIONS

Warm oil on Sauté. Add in onion and garlic and cook for 2 minutes until softened. Stir in sausage meat and cook for 5 minutes. Stir in jalapeño, water, sun-dried tomatoes, Italian seasoning, oregano, diced tomatoes, and salt with the chicken; mix spaghetti and press to submerge into the sauce.

Seal the lid and cook on High Pressure for 9 minutes. Release the Pressure quickly. Stir in spinach, close lid again, and simmer on Keep Warm for 5 minutes until spinach is wilted.

Gouda Beef Fettuccine

Servings: 6 | Prep + Cook Time: 20 minutes

INGREDIENTS

10 oz ground beef
1 lb fettuccine pasta
1 cup gouda cheese, shredded
1 cup fresh spinach, torn
1 medium onion, chopped

2 cups tomatoes, diced
1 tbsp butter
1 tsp salt
½ tsp ground black pepper

DIRECTIONS

Melt butter on Sauté. Stir-fry the beef and onion for 5 minutes. Add the pasta. Pour water enough to cover and season with salt and pepper. Cook on High Pressure for 5 minutes.

Do a quick release. Press Sauté and stir in the tomato and spinach; cook for 5 minutes. Top with Gouda to serve.

Minestrone with Pesto & Rigatoni

Servings: 4 | Prep + Cook Time: 15 minutes

INGREDIENTS

3 tbsp olive oil
1 onion, diced
1 celery stalk, diced
1 large carrot, peeled and diced
14 ounces canned chopped tomatoes
4 ounces rigatoni
3 cups water
1 cup chopped zucchini

1 bay leaf
1 tsp mixed herbs
¼ tsp cayenne pepper
½ tsp salt
¼ cup shredded Pecorino Romano cheese
1 garlic clove, minced
⅓ cup olive oil based pesto

DIRECTIONS

Heat oil on Sauté and cook onion, celery, garlic, and carrot for 3 minutes, stirring occasionally until the vegetables are softened. Stir in rigatoni, tomatoes, water, zucchini, bay leaf, herbs, cayenne, and salt.

Seal the lid and cook on High for 4 minutes. Do a natural pressure release for 5 minutes. Adjust the taste of the soup with salt and black pepper, and remove the bay leaf.

Ladle the soup into serving bowls and drizzle the pesto over. Serve with the garlic toasts.

Creamy Primavera Farfalle

Servings: 4 | Prep + Cook Time: 20 minutes

INGREDIENTS

1 bunch asparagus, trimmed, cut into 1-inch pieces
2 cups broccoli florets
3 tbsp olive oil
3 tsp salt
10 ounces egg noodles
3 garlic cloves, minced
2 ½ cups vegetable stock
½ cup heavy cream
1 cup small tomatoes, halved
¼ cup chopped basil
½ cup grated Parmesan cheese

DIRECTIONS

Pour 2 cups of water, add the noodles, 2 tbsp of olive oil, garlic and salt. Place a trivet over the water. Combine asparagus, broccoli, remaining olive oil and salt in a bowl. Place the vegetables on the trivet.

Seal the lid and cook on Steam for 12 minutes on High. Do a quick release. Remove the vegetables to a plate. Stir the heavy cream and tomatoes in the pasta. Press Sauté and simmer the cream until desired consistency. Gently mix in the asparagus and broccoli. Garnish with basil and Parmesan, to serve.

Quattro Formaggi Tagliatelle

Servings: 6 | Prep + Cook Time: 15 minutes

INGREDIENTS

¼ cup goat's cheese, chevre
¼ cup grated Pecorino cheese
½ cup grated Parmesan
1 cup heavy cream
½ cup grated Gouda
¼ cup butter, softened
1 tbsp Italian Seasoning mix
1 cup vegetable broth
1 lb tagliatelle

DIRECTIONS

In a bowl, mix goat cheese, pecorino, parmesan, and heavy cream. Stir in Italian seasoning. Transfer to your instant pot. Stir in the broth and butter.

Seal the lid and cook on High Pressure for 4 minutes. Do a quick release. Meanwhile, drop the tagliatelle in boiling water and cook for 6 minutes.

Remove the instant pot's lid and stir in the tagliatelle. Top with grated gouda and let simmer for about 10 minutes on Sauté mode.

POULTRY

Thyme Chicken with Veggies

Servings: 4 | Prep + Cook Time: 40 minutes

INGREDIENTS

4 skin-on, bone-in chicken legs
2 tbsp olive oil
Salt and freshly ground black pepper to taste
4 cloves garlic, minced
1 tsp fresh chopped thyme
½ cup dry white wine
1¼ cups chicken stock

1 cup carrots, thinly chopped
1 cup parsnip, thinly chopped
3 tomatoes, thinly chopped
1 tbsp honey
4 slices lemon
Fresh thyme, chopped for garnish

DIRECTIONS

Season the chicken with pepper and salt. Warm oil on Sauté mode.

Arrange chicken legs into the hot oil; cook for 3 to 5 minutes each side until browned. Place in a bowl and set aside. Sauté thyme and garlic in the chicken fat for 1 minute until soft and lightly golden.

Add wine into the pot to deglaze, scrape the pot's bottom to get rid of any brown bits of food. Simmer the wine for 2 to 3 minutes until slightly reduced in volume.

Add stock, carrots, parsnips, tomatoes, pepper and salt into the pot. Lay steam rack onto veggies.

Into the pressure cooker's steamer basket, arrange chicken legs. Set the steamer basket onto the rack.

Drizzle the chicken with honey then Top with lemon slices.

Seal the lid and cook on High Pressure for 12 minutes. Release Pressure naturally for 10 minutes.

Place the chicken to a bowl. Drain the veggies and place them around the chicken. Garnish with fresh thyme leaves before serving.

Chicken with Tomatoes & Capers

Servings: 4 | Prep + Cook Time: 45 minutes

INGREDIENTS

4 chicken legs
Sea salt and black pepper to taste
2 tbsp olive oil
1 onion, diced
2 garlic cloves, minced

⅓ cup red wine
2 cups diced tomatoes
⅓ cup capers
¼ cup fresh basil
2 pickles, chopped

DIRECTIONS

Sprinkle pepper and salt over the chicken. Warm oil on Sauté. Add in onion and Sauté for 3 minutes until fragrant. Add in garlic and cook for 30 seconds until softened.

Mix the chicken with vegetables and cook for 6 to 7 minutes until lightly browned.

Add red wine to the pan to deglaze, scrape the pan's bottom to get rid of any browned bits of food; Stir in tomatoes. Seal the lid and cook on High Pressure for 12 minutes. Release the Pressure quickly.

To the chicken mixture, add basil, capers and pickles. Serve the chicken topped with the tomato sauce mixture.

Herby Chicken with Asparagus Sauce

Servings: 4 | Prep + Cook Time: 1 hour

INGREDIENTS

- 1 (3 ½ pounds) Young Whole Chicken
- 4 garlic cloves, minced
- 1 tsp olive oil
- 4 fresh thyme, minced
- 3 fresh rosemary, minced
- 2 lemons, zested and quartered
- Salt and freshly ground black pepper to taste
- 2 tbsp olive oil
- 8 ounces asparagus, trimmed and chopped
- 1 onion, chopped
- 1 cup chicken stock
- 1 tbsp soy sauce
- 1 fresh thyme sprig
- Cooking spray
- 1 tbsp flour
- Chopped parsley to garnish

DIRECTIONS

Rub all sides of the chicken with garlic, rosemary, black pepper, lemon zest, thyme, and salt. Into the chicken cavity, insert lemon wedges. Warm oil on Sauté. Add in onion and asparagus, and sauté for 5 minutes until softened. Mix chicken stock, 1 thyme sprig, black pepper, soy sauce, and salt.

Into the inner pot, set trivet over asparagus mixture. On top of the trivet, place the chicken with breast-side up.

Seal the lid, select Poultry and cook for 20 minutes on High Pressure. Do a quick release. Remove the chicken to a serving platter.

In the inner pot, sprinkle flour over asparagus mixture and blend the sauce with an immersion blender until desired consistency. Top the chicken with asparagus sauce and garnish with parsley.

Greek-Style Chicken with Potatoes

Servings: 4 | Prep + Cook Time: 40 minutes

INGREDIENTS

- 4 potatoes, peeled and quartered
- 4 cups water
- 2 lemons, zested and juiced
- 1 tbsp olive oil
- 2 tsp fresh oregano
- Salt to taste
- ¼ tsp freshly ground black pepper
- 2 Serrano peppers, stemmed, cored, and chopped
- 4 boneless skinless chicken drumsticks
- 3 tbsp finely chopped parsley
- 1 cup packed watercress
- 1 cucumber, thinly chopped
- ½ cup cherry tomatoes, quartered
- ¼ cup Kalamata olives, pitted
- ¼ cup hummus
- ¼ cup feta cheese, crumbled
- Lemon wedges, for serving

DIRECTIONS

In the cooker, add water and potatoes. Set trivet over them. In a baking bowl, mix lemon juice, olive oil, black pepper, oregano, zest, salt, and red pepper flakes. Add chicken drumsticks in the marinade and stir to coat.

Set the bowl with chicken on the trivet in the inner pot. Seal the lid, select Poultry and cook on High for 15 minutes. Do a quick release. Take out the bowl with chicken and the trivet from the pot. Drain potatoes and add parsley and salt.

Split the potatoes among four serving plates and top with watercress, cucumber slices, hummus, cherry tomatoes, chicken, olives, and feta cheese. Each bowl should be garnished with a lemon wedge.

Lettuce Chicken Wraps

Servings: 6 | Prep + Cook Time: 50 minutes

INGREDIENTS

2 tbsp canola oil
2 pounds chicken thighs, boneless, skinless
1 cup pineapple juice
⅓ cup water
¼ cup soy sauce
2 tbsp maple syrup

1 tbsp rice vinegar
1 tsp chili-garlic sauce
3 tbsp cornstarch
Salt and freshly ground black pepper to taste
12 large lettuce leaves
2 cups canned pinto beans, rinsed and drained

DIRECTIONS

Warm oil on Sauté. In batches, sear chicken in the oil for 5 minutes until browned. Set aside in a bowl.

Into your pot, mix chili-garlic sauce, pineapple juice, soy sauce, vinegar, maple syrup, and water; Stir in chicken to coat. Seal the lid and cook on High Pressure for 7 minutes. Release Pressure naturally for 10 minutes. Shred the chicken with two forks. Take ¼ cup liquid from the pot to a bowl; Stir in cornstarch to dissolve.

Mix the cornstarch mixture with the mixture in the pot and return the chicken.

Select Sauté and cook for 5 minutes until the sauce thickens; add pepper and salt for seasoning.

Transfer beans into lettuce leaves, top with chicken carnitas and serve.

Paprika Buttered Chicken

Servings: 6 | Prep + Cook Time: 45 minutes

INGREDIENTS

1 cup chicken stock
½ cup white wine
½ onion, thinly chopped
2 cloves garlic, minced
3.5-pound whole chicken, patted dry with paper towel

1 tsp salt
½ tsp ground black pepper
½ tsp dried thyme
3 tbsp butter, melted
½ tsp paprika

DIRECTIONS

Into the pot, add onion, chicken stock, white wine, and garlic. Over the mixture, place a steamer rack.

Rub pepper, salt, and thyme onto chicken; lay onto the rack breast-side up. Seal the lid, press Poultry and cook on High Pressure for 26 minutes. Release the Pressure quickly.

While pressure releases, preheat oven broiler. In a bowl, mix paprika and butter. Remove the rack with chicken from your pot. Get rid of onion and stock. Onto the chicken, brush butter mixture and take the rack back to the pot. Cook under the broiler for 5 minutes until chicken skin is crispy and browned.

Set chicken to a cutting board to cool for about 5 minutes, then carve and transfer to a serving platter.

Spicy Salsa Chicken with Feta

Servings: 6 | Prep + Cook Time: 30 minutes

INGREDIENTS

2 pounds boneless skinless chicken drumsticks
¼ tsp salt
1 ½ cups hot tomato salsa

1 onion, chopped
1 cup feta cheese, crumbled

DIRECTIONS

Sprinkle salt over the chicken; and set in the instant pot. Stir in salsa to coat the chicken. Seal the lid and cook for 15 minutes on High Pressure. Do a quick Pressure release. Press Sauté and cook for 5-10 minutes as you stir until excess liquid has evaporated. Top with feta cheese to serve.

Chicken Cacciatore

Servings: 4 | Prep + Cook Time: 40 minutes

INGREDIENTS

2 tsp olive oil
1 pound chicken drumsticks, boneless, skinless
2 tsp salt
1½ tsp freshly ground black pepper
1 carrot, chopped
1 red bell pepper, chopped
1 yellow bell pepper, chopped
1 onion, chopped
4 garlic cloves, minced

2 tsp dried oregano
1 tsp dried basil
1 tsp dried parsley
1 pinch red pepper flakes
1 (28-ounce) can diced tomatoes
½ cup dry red wine
¾ cup chicken stock
1 cup black olives, pitted and chopped
2 bay leaves

DIRECTIONS

Warm oil on Sauté mode. Season the drumsticks with pepper and salt. In batches, sear the chicken for 5-6 minutes until golden-brown. Set aside on a plate. Drain the pot and remain with 1 tablespoon of fat.

In the hot oil, Sauté onion, garlic, and bell peppers for 4 minutes until softened; add red pepper flakes, basil, parsley, and oregano, and cook for 30 more seconds. Season with salt and pepper.

Stir in tomatoes, olives, chicken stock, red wine and bay leaves.

Return chicken to the pot. Seal the lid and cook on High Pressure for 15 minutes. Release the Pressure quickly. Divide chicken into four serving bowls; Top with tomato mixture before serving.

Creamy Chicken Pasta with Pesto Sauce

Servings: 8 | Prep + Cook Time: 30 minutes

INGREDIENTS

3½ cups water
4 chicken breast, boneless, skinless, cubed
8 oz macaroni pasta
1 tbsp butter
1 tablespoon salt, divided
2 cups fresh collard greens, trimmed
1 cup cherry tomatoes, halved

½ cup basil pesto sauce
¼ cup cream cheese, at room temperature
1 garlic clove, minced
1 tsp freshly ground black pepper to taste
¼ cup Asiago cheese, grated
Freshly chopped basil for garnish

DIRECTIONS

Add water, chicken, 2 tsp salt, butter, and macaroni, and stir well to mix and be submerged in water.

Seal the lid and cook for 2 minutes on High Pressure. Release the Pressure quickly.

Press Cancel, open the lid, get rid of ¼ cup water from the pot.

Set on Sauté mode. Into the pot, mix in collard greens, pesto sauce, garlic, remaining 1 teaspoon salt, cream cheese, tomatoes, and black pepper. Cook, for 1 to 2 minutes as you stir, until sauce is creamy. Place the pasta into serving plates. Top with asiago cheese and basil before serving.

Pesto Stuffed Chicken with Green Beans

Servings: 4 | Prep + Cook Time: 20 minutes

INGREDIENTS

4 chicken breasts
1 tbsp butter
1 tbsp olive oil
¼ cup dry white wine

For pesto:
1 cup fresh basil
1 garlic clove, smashed
2 tbsp. pine nuts

¾ cup chicken stock
1 tsp salt
1 cup green beans, trimmed and cut into 1-inch pieces

¼ cup Parmesan Cheese
¼ cup extra virgin olive oil

DIRECTIONS

First make the pesto - in a bowl, mix fresh basil, pine nuts, garlic, salt, pepper and Parmesan and place in food processor. Add in oil and process until the desired consistency is attained.

Apply a thin layer of pesto to one side of each chicken breast; tightly roll into a cylinder and fasten closed with small skewers. Press Sauté. Add oil and butter. Cook chicken rolls for 1 to 2 minutes per side until browned.

Add in wine and cook until the wine has evaporated, about 3-4 minutes.

Add stock and salt, and top the chicken with green beans. Seal the lid, press Meat/Stew and cook at High Pressure for 5 minutes. Release the Pressure quickly.

Serve chicken rolls with cooking liquid and green beans.

Italian Chicken Thighs with Mushrooms

Servings: 2 | Prep + Cook Time: 30 minutes

INGREDIENTS

2 chicken thighs, boneless and skinless
6 oz button mushrooms
3 tbsp olive oil
1 tsp fresh rosemary, finely chopped

2 garlic cloves, crushed
½ tsp salt
1 tbsp butter
1 tbsp Italian Seasoning mix

DIRECTIONS

Heat a tablespoon of olive oil on Sauté. Add chicken thighs and sear for 5 minutes. Set aside. Pour in the remaining oil, and add mushrooms, rosemary, and Italian seasoning mix. Stir-fry for 5 minutes.

Add in butter, chicken, and 2 cups of water. Seal the lid and cook on Pressure Cook mode for 13 minutes on High. Do a quick release. Remove the chicken and mushrooms from the cooker and serve with onions.

Chicken in Orange Gravy

Servings: 4 | Prep + Cook Time: 25 minutes

INGREDIENTS

1 tbsp olive oil
4 boneless, skinless chicken thighs,
¼ cup orange juice
2 tbsp ketchup
2 tbsp Worcestershire sauce

1 garlic clove, minced
1 tsp cornstarch
2 tsp water
A handful of fresh cilantro, chopped

DIRECTIONS

Warm oil on Sauté. In batches, sear chicken in oil for 3 minutes until golden brown; set aside on a plate.

Mix orange juice, Worcestershire sauce, garlic, and ketchup; add to the pot to deglaze, scrape the bottom to get rid of any browned bits of food. Place the chicken into the sauce and stir well to coat. Seal the lid cook for 5 minutes on High Pressure. Release the Pressure quickly.

In a small bowl, mix water and cornstarch until well dissolved. Press Cancel and set to Sauté mode. Stir the cornstarch slurry into the sauce; cook for 2 minutes until the sauce is well thickened. Serve in bowls with cilantro.

Turkey with Rigatoni

Servings: 4 | Prep + Cook Time: 40 minutes

INGREDIENTS

2 tbsp canola oil
1 pound ground turkey
1 egg
¼ cup bread crumbs
2 cloves garlic, minced

1 tsp dried oregano
Salt and ground black pepper to taste
3 cups tomato sauce
ounces rigatoni
2 tbsp grated Grana Padano cheese

DIRECTIONS

In a bowl, combine turkey, crumbs, cumin, garlic, and egg. Season with oregano, salt, red pepper flakes, and pepper. Form the mixture into meatballs with well-oiled hands.

Warm the oil on Sauté. Cook the meatballs for 3 to 4 minutes, until browned on all sides. Remove to a plate.

Add rigatoni to the cooker and cover with tomato sauce. Pour enough water to cover the pasta. Stir well. Throw in the meatballs. Seal the lid and cook for 10 minutes on High Pressure. Release the Pressure quickly. Serve topped with Grana Padano cheese.

Greek Turkey Meatballs

Servings: 6 | Prep + Cook Time: 30 minutes

INGREDIENTS

1 onion, minced
½ cup plain bread crumbs
⅓ cup feta cheese, crumbled
2 tsp salt
½ tsp dried oregano
¼ tsp ground black pepper
1 pound ground turkey

1 egg, lightly beaten
1 tbsp olive oil
1 carrot, minced
½ celery stalk, minced
3 cups tomato puree
2 cups water

DIRECTIONS

In a mixing bowl, combine half the onion, oregano, turkey, salt, crumbs, pepper, and egg, and stir until everything is well incorporated.

Heat oil on Sauté mode, and cook celery, remaining onion, and carrot for 5 minutes, until soft. Pour in water, and tomato puree. Adjust the seasonings.

Roll the mixture into meatballs, and drop into the sauce. Seal the lid.

Press Meat/Stew and cook on High Pressure for 5 minutes. Allow the cooker to cool and release the pressure naturally for 20 minutes. Serve topped with feta cheese.

Chicken with Salsa Verde

Servings: 4 | Prep + Cook Time: 50 minutes

INGREDIENTS

Salsa Verde:
1 jalapeño pepper, deveined and chopped
½ cup capers
¼ cup parsley

1 Lime, juiced
1 tsp salt
¼ cup extra virgin olive oil

Chicken:
4 boneless skinless chicken breasts
2 cups water

1 cup rice, rinsed

DIRECTIONS

In a blender, mix olive oil, salt, lime juice, jalapeño pepper, capers, and parsley and blend until smooth. Arrange chicken breasts at the bottom of the cooker. Over the chicken, add salsa verde mixture.

In a bowl that can fit in the cooker, mix rice and water. Set a steamer rack onto chicken and sauce. Set the bowl onto the rack. Seal the lid and cook on High Pressure for 20 minutes. Release the Pressure quickly.

Remove the rice bowl and rack. Using two forks, shred chicken into the sauce; stir to coat. Divide the rice, between plates. Top with chicken and salsa verde before serving.

Chicken Meatballs in Tomato Sauce

Servings: 5 | Prep + Cook Time: 35 minutes

INGREDIENTS

1 pound ground chicken
3 tbsp red hot sauce
1 egg
⅓ cup crumbled blue cheese
¼ cup bread crumbs
¼ cup Pecorino cheese
1 tbsp ranch dressing

1 tsp dried basil
Salt and ground black pepper to taste
15 ounces canned tomato sauce
1 cup chicken broth
2 tbsp olive oil
A handful of parsley, chopped

DIRECTIONS

In a bowl, mix chicken, egg, pecorino, basil, pepper, salt, ranch dressing, blue cheese, 3 tbsp hot sauce, and bread crumbs; shape the mixture into meatballs.

Warm oil on Sauté mode. Add in the meatballs and cook for 2 to 3 minutes until browned on all sides.

Add in tomato sauce and broth. Seal the lid and cook on High Pressure for 7 minutes. Release the pressure quickly. Remove meatballs carefully and place to a serving plate. Top with parsley and serve.

Chicken with Steamed Artichokes

Servings: 3 | Prep + Cook Time: 35 minutes

INGREDIENTS

1 lb chicken breasts, boneless, skinless, chopped
2 artichokes, trimmed, halved
2 tbsp butter, melted

2 tbsp olive oil
1 lemon, juiced
Himalayan salt and black pepper to taste

DIRECTIONS

Heat oil on Sauté and cook the chicken for a minute per side, until golden. Pour in 1 cup of water, seal the lid, and cook on High pressure for 13 minutes. Do a quick release. Set aside the chicken.

Place the trivet and pour a cup of water. Rub the artichoke halves with half of the lemon juice, and arrange on top of the trivet. Seal the lid and cook on Steam for 3 minutes on High. Do a quick release.

Combine artichoke and chicken in a large bowl. Stir in salt, pepper, and lemon juice. Drizzle butter over.

Valencian Chicken Paella

Servings: 4 | Prep + Cook Time: 30 minutes

INGREDIENTS

4 boneless, skinless chicken legs
1 garlic clove, minced
½ tsp paprika
½ tsp turmeric
1 tsp cayenne pepper
1 tsp ground white pepper
Salt to taste
1 tbsp oil olive

1 onion, chopped
1 tbsp tomato puree
2 cups chicken broth
1 cup long grain rice
1 celery stalk, diced
1 cup frozen green peas
1 red bell pepper, chopped
Fresh parsley for garnish

DIRECTIONS

Season chicken with garlic powder, white pepper, paprika, cayenne pepper, and salt.

Warm the oil on Sauté. Add in onion, garlic, and bell pepper; cook for 5 minutes. Mix in tomato puree.

Add ¼ cup chicken stock into the cooker to deglaze the pan, scrape the pan's bottom to get rid of browned bits of food.

Mix in celery, rice, and the chicken. Add in the remaining broth. Seal the lid and cook on High Pressure for 8 minutes. Do a quick release. Mix in green peas, cover with the lid and let sit for 5 minutes. Serve warm.

Hot Chicken with Black Beans

Servings: 4 | Prep + Cook Time: 25 minutes

INGREDIENTS

½ cup chicken broth
3 tbsp honey
2 tbsp tomato paste
½ cup hot sauce
3 garlic cloves, grated
4 boneless, skinless chicken drumsticks

1 tbsp cornstarch
1 tbsp water
1 tbsp olive oil
2 cups canned black beans
2 green onions, thinly chopped

DIRECTIONS

In the cooker, mix the hot sauce, honey, tomato paste, chicken broth, and garlic. Stir well until smooth; toss in the chicken to coat.

Seal the lid and cook for 3 minutes on High Pressure. Release the Pressure immediately.

Open the lid and press Sauté. In a small bowl, mix water and cornstarch until no lumps remain, Stir into the sauce and cook for 5 minutes until thickened.

Stir in olive oil and black beans; garnish with green onions and serve.

Chicken Risotto with Vegetables

Servings: 4 | Prep + Cook Time: 65 minutes

INGREDIENTS

10 oz chicken breasts, boneless, skinless, cut into pieces
1 cup rice
6 oz button mushrooms, chopped, stems removed
1 red bell pepper, halved, seeds removed
1 green bell pepper, halved, seeds removed
1 yellow bell pepper, halved, seeds removed
6 oz broccoli, cut into florets
½ cup sweet corn

2 carrots, peeled and chopped
2 tbsp olive oil
1 tbsp butter
1 tsp salt
½ tsp freshly ground black pepper
1 tsp fresh basil, finely chopped
Parmesan Cheese for topping

DIRECTIONS

Add rice and pour in 3 cups of water. Stir in butter, pepper and salt and seal the lid. Cook on Rice mode for 8 minutes on High. Do a quick release and remove the rice.

Heat oil on Sauté, and add carrots and broccoli. Sauté for 10 minutes. Add sweet corn and bell peppers and cook for 5 minutes, stirring constantly. Finally, stir in mushrooms, and cook for 3-4 minutes.

Remove the vegetables, mix with rice and set aside. Add the chicken to the pot and pour in 2 cups of water. Season with salt and pepper. Seal the lid and cook on High pressure for 7 minutes.

Do a quick release. Open the lid, stir in rice and vegetables and serve warm sprinkled with Parmesan.

Spicy Mushroom Chicken

Servings: 3 | Prep + Cook Time: 25 minutes

INGREDIENTS

1 lb chicken breasts, skinless, boneless, cut into pieces
1 cup button mushrooms, chopped
2 cups chicken broth
2 tbsp flour
1 tsp cayenne pepper, ground

1 tsp salt
1 tbsp olive oil
2 garlic cloves, chopped
¼ tsp freshly ground black pepper

DIRECTIONS

Grease the inner pot with oil. Add garlic and meat, Season with salt, and stir-fry for 3 minutes. Add mushrooms and pour the chicken broth. Seal the lid.

Cook on High Pressure for 8 minutes. Release the steam naturally, for 10 minutes and stir in flour, cayenne, and black pepper. Stir-fry for 5 more minutes, on Sauté mode. Serve warm.

Mediterranean Chicken

Servings: 2 | Prep + Cook Time: 20 minutes

INGREDIENTS

1 lb chicken breast, cut into ½ -inch thick slices
1 cup olive oil
1 cup chicken broth
½ cup freshly squeezed lemon juice
½ cup parsley leaves, chopped

3 garlic cloves, crushed
1 tbsp cayenne pepper
1 tsp dried oregano
½ tsp kosher salt

DIRECTIONS

In a bowl, mix olive oil, lemon juice, parsley, garlic, cayenne, oregano, and salt. Submerge fillets in this mixture and cover. Chill for 30 minutes. Remove from the fridge and place all inside the pot. Add in the broth.

Seal the lid and cook on High Pressure for 7 minutes. Release the Pressure naturally, for about 10 minutes and serve immediately.

Herbed Chicken Thighs

Servings: 4 | Prep + Cook Time: 1 hour 30 minutes

INGREDIENTS

4 chicken thighs
1 cup chicken broth
1 cup olive oil
¼ cup apple cider vinegar
3 garlic cloves, crushed
½ cup freshly squeezed lemon juice

1 tbsp fresh basil, chopped
2 tbsp fresh thyme, chopped
1 tbsp fresh rosemary, chopped
1 tsp cayenne pepper
1 tsp salt

DIRECTIONS

In a bowl, add oil, vinegar, garlic, juice, basil, thyme, rosemary, salt, and cayenne. Submerge thighs into this mixture and refrigerate for one hour. Remove from the fridge and pat dry with kitchen paper.

Pour the broth in the pot. Set the trivet and place the chicken on it. Seal the lid and cook on Steam mode for 15 minutes on High. Do a quick release and remove the chicken and broth; wipe clean.

Press Sauté, warm oil and brown the chicken thighs for 5 minutes, turning once, until nice and golden.

Lemon & Mustard Chicken

Servings: 2 | Prep + Cook Time: 35 minutes

INGREDIENTS

1 lb chicken breasts, boneless and skinless
¼ cup apple cider vinegar
1 tsp garlic powder
2 tbsp Dijon mustard

¼ tsp black pepper, freshly ground
2 tbsp olive oil
2 cups chicken stock

DIRECTIONS

Season the meat with garlic and black pepper. Place in the instant pot and pour in the stock. Seal the lid and cook on Poultry mode for 20 minutes on High.

Do a quick release and remove the meat along with the stock. In a bowl, mix olive oil, dijon, and apple cider. Pour into the pot and press Sauté.

Place the meat in this mixture and cook for 10 minutes, turning once. When done, remove from the pot and drizzle with the sauce.

Italian-Style Turkey with Vegetables

Servings: 4 | Prep + Cook Time: 45 minutes

INGREDIENTS

- 1 lb turkey breast, chopped into bite-sized pieces
- 1 tsp red pepper flakes
- 2 cups canned tomatoes, diced
- 3 cups chicken broth
- 1 tsp honey
- 2 cups zucchini, cubed
- 3 garlic cloves, chopped
- 1 cup onions, finely chopped
- 2 tbsp tomato paste
- 1 cup baby carrots, chopped
- Salt and pepper to taste
- 2 tbsp olive oil

INSTRUCTIONS:

Mix all ingredients in your instant pot. Seal the lid and cook on Meat/Stew mode for 25 minutes on High Pressure. When ready, do a quick release and open the lid. Serve immediately.

Turkey Patties

Servings: 4 | Prep + Cook Time: 25 minutes

INGREDIENTS

- 1 lb ground turkey
- 2 eggs
- 1 cup flour
- 1 onion, finely chopped
- 2 tsp dried dill, chopped
- ½ tsp salt
- ½ tsp black pepper, ground
- 1 cup sour cream

DIRECTIONS

In a bowl, add all ingredients and mix well with hands. Form the patties with the previously prepared mixture. Line parchment paper over a baking dish and arrange the patties. Pour 1 cup of water in the pot.

Lay the trivet and place the baking dish on top. Seal the lid. Cook on Pressure Cook mode for 15 minutes on High. Release the pressure naturally, for 10 minutes. Serve with lettuce and tomatoes.

Turkey Pepperoni Pizza

Servings: 4 | Prep + Cook Time: 25 minutes

INGREDIENTS

- 1 whole wheat Italian pizza crust
- 1 cup fire-roasted tomatoes, diced
- 1 tsp oregano
- ½ tsp dried basil
- ½ cup turkey pepperoni, chopped
- 7 oz Gouda cheese, grated
- 2 tbsp olive oil

DIRECTIONS

Grease a baking pan with oil. Line some parchment paper and place the pizza crust in it.

Spread the fire-roasted tomatoes over the pizza crust and sprinkle with oregano and basil. Make a layer with cheese and top with pepperoni.

Add a trivet inside the pot and pour in 1 cup of water. Seal the lid, and cook for 15 minutes on High Pressure. Do a quick release. Remove the pizza from the pot using a parchment paper.

Roast Turkey with Basil and Garlic

Servings: 6 | Prep + Cook Time: 50 minutes

INGREDIENTS

2 lb boneless turkey breast, halved
2 garlic cloves, crushed
1 tsp dried basil
1 tsp white pepper
3 whole cloves

½ cup soy sauce
½ cup lemon juice
1 tbsp cane sugar
¼ cup oil
3 cups chicken broth

DIRECTIONS

Place the meat in a ziploc bag and add basil, cloves, soy sauce, oil, and lemon juice. Pour in 1 cup of broth and Seal. Shake and Refrigerate for 30 minutes.

Heat oil on Sauté and stir-fry the garlic for 2 minutes. Add in the along with 2 tbsp of the marinade and the remaining broth. Seal the lid.

Cook on Poultry for 25 minutes on High. Release the Pressure naturally, for 10 minutes.

Italian-Style Chicken Stew

Servings: 4 | Prep + Cook Time: 20 minutes

INGREDIENTS

2 lb chicken wings
2 potatoes, peeled, cut into chunks
2 fire-roasted tomatoes, peeled, chopped
1 carrot, peeled, cut into chunks
2 garlic cloves, chopped
2 tbsp olive oil

1 tsp smoked paprika, ground
4 cups chicken broth
2 tbsp fresh parsley, chopped
1 tsp salt
¼ tsp black pepper, ground
1 cup spinach, chopped

DIRECTIONS

Rub the chicken with salt, pepper, and paprika, and place in the pot. Add in all remaining ingredients and seal the lid. Cook on High Pressure for 8 minutes. When ready, do a quick release. Serve hot.

Chicken in Garlic Yogurt Sauce

Servings: 6 | Prep + Cook Time: 42 minutes

INGREDIENTS

12 chicken wings
3 tbsp olive oil

Yogurt sauce:
½ cup sour cream
1 cup yogurt

1 tsp salt
3 cups chicken broth

2 garlic cloves, peeled and crushed

DIRECTIONS

Heat oil on Sauté. Brown the wings for 6-8 minutes, turning once. Pour in the broth and seal the lid. Cook on Poultry mode for 15 minutes on High Pressure. Do a natural release, for about 10 minutes.

In a bowl, mix sour cream, yogurt and garlic. Chill the wings for a while and drizzle with yogurt sauce.

PORK

Pork Chops & Broccoli with Gravy

Servings: 6 | Prep + Cook Time: 45 minutes

INGREDIENTS

PORK CHOPS:

1 ½ tsp salt
1 tsp ground black pepper
1 tsp garlic powder
1 tsp onion powder
1 tsp red pepper flakes

6 boneless pork chops
1 broccoli head, broken into florets
1 cup chicken stock
¼ cup butter, melted
¼ cup milk

GRAVY:

3 tbsp flour
½ cup heavy cream

Salt and ground black pepper to taste

DIRECTIONS

Combine salt, garlic powder, flakes, onion, and black pepper. Rub the mixture onto pork chops. Place stock and broccoli in the instant pot. Lay the pork chops on top.

Seal the lid and cook for 15 minutes on High Pressure. Release the Pressure quickly.

Transfer the pork chops and broccoli to a plate. Press Sauté and simmer the liquid remaining in the pot.

Mix cream and flour. Pour into the simmering liquid and cook for 4 to 6 minutes until thickened and bubbly. Season with pepper and salt. Top the chops with gravy, drizzle butter over broccoli and serve.

Italian Sausage & Cannellini Stew

Servings: 6 | Prep + Cook Time: 45 minutes

INGREDIENTS

1 tbsp olive oil
1 pound Italian sausages, halved
1 celery stalk, chopped
1 carrot, chopped
1 onion, chopped
1 sprig fresh sage

1 sprig fresh rosemary
1 bay leaf
1 cup Cannellini beans, soaked and rinsed
2 cups vegetable stock
3 cups fresh spinach
1 tsp salt

DIRECTIONS

Warm oil on Sauté. Add in sausage pieces and sear for 5 minutes until browned; set aside on a plate.

To the pot, add celery, onion, bay leaf, sage, carrot, and rosemary; cook for 3 minutes to soften slightly.

Stir in vegetable stock and beans. Arrange seared sausage pieces on top of the beans.

Seal the lid, press Bean/Chili and cook on High for 10 minutes. Release Pressure naturally for 20 minutes, do a quick release. Get rid of bay leaf, rosemary and sage. Mix spinach into the mixture to serve.

Sausage with Celeriac & Potato Mash

Servings: 4 | Prep + Cook Time: 45 minutes

INGREDIENTS

1 tbsp olive oil
4 pork sausages
1 onion
2 cups vegetable broth
½ cup water
4 potatoes, peeled and diced
1 cup celeriac, chopped

2 tbsp butter
¼ cup milk
Salt and ground black pepper to taste
1 tbsp heavy cream
1 tsp Dijon mustard
½ tsp dry mustard powder
Fresh flat-leaf parsley, chopped

DIRECTIONS

Warm oil on Sauté mode. Add in sausages and cook for 1 to 2 minutes for each side until browned. Set the sausages to a plate. To the same pot, add onion and sauté for 3 minutes until fragrant. Press Cancel.

Add sausages on top of onions and pour water and broth over them. Place a trivet over onions and sausages. Put potatoes and celeriac in a steamer basket and transfer it to the trivet.

Seal the lid and cook for 11 minutes on High Pressure. Release the pressure quickly. Transfer potatoes and celeriac to a bowl and set sausages on a plate and cover them with aluminum foil.

Using a potato masher, mash potatoes and celeriac together with black pepper, milk, salt and butter until mash becomes creamy and fluffy. Adjust the seasonings.

Set on Sauté mode. Add the onion mixture and bring to a boil. Cook for 5 to 10 minutes until the mixture is reduced and thickened. Into the gravy, stir in dry mustard, salt, pepper, mustard and cream.

Place the mash in 4 bowls in equal parts, top with a sausage or two, and gravy. Garnish with parsley.

Pork Chops with Squash Purée & Mushroom Gravy

Servings: 4 | Prep + Cook Time: 45 minutes

INGREDIENTS

3 tbsp olive oil
2 sprigs thyme, leaves removed and chopped
2 sprigs rosemary, leaves removed and chopped
4 pork chops
1 cup mushrooms, chopped
4 cloves garlic, minced

1 cup chicken broth
1 tbsp soy sauce
1 pound butternut squash, cubed
1 tbsp olive oil
1 tsp cornstarch

DIRECTIONS

Set on Sauté and heat rosemary, thyme and 2 tbsp of oil. Add the pork chops and sear for 1 minute for each side until lightly browned.

Sauté garlic and mushrooms in the instant pot for 5-6 minutes until mushrooms are tender. Add soy sauce and broth. Transfer pork chops to a wire trivet and place it into the pot. Over the chops, place a cake pan. Add butternut squash in the pot and drizzle with 1 tbsp olive oil.

Seal the lid and cook on High Pressure for 10 minutes. Release the pressure quickly. Remove the pan and trivet from the pot. Stir cornstarch into the mushroom mixture for 2 to 3 minutes until the sauce thickens.

Transfer the mushroom sauce to an immersion blender and blend until you attain the desired consistency. Scoop sauce into a cup with a pour spout. Smash the squash into a purée. Set pork chops on a plate and ladle squash puree next to them. Top the pork chops with gravy.

Italian Tomato Glazes Pork Meatloaf

Prep + Cook Time: 30 minutes | Servings: 4

FOR THE MEATLOAF:

2 pounds ground pork
2 garlic cloves, minced
1 cup breadcrumbs
1 large-sized egg
1 cup milk

2 small onions, finely chopped
Salt and cracked black pepper, to taste
½ tsp turmeric powder
½ tsp dried oregano
Cooking spray, for greasing

For the Topping:

1 cup ketchup
2 tbsp brown sugar
¼ cup tomato paste

1 tsp garlic powder
½ tsp onion powder
½ tsp cayenne Pepper

DIRECTIONS

Place the trivet at the bottom of your pressure cooker and pour 1 cup of water. Lightly grease a round sheet pan, that fits in your pressure cooker.

Mix ground pork, bread crumbs, milk, onion, egg, salt, black pepper, oregano, and thyme in a mixing bowl. Use your hands to combine thoroughly. Shape into a loaf and place onto the prepared sheet pan.

In another bowl, mix the ingredients for the topping. Spread the topping over the meatloaf and lower the sheet pan onto the trivet. Seal the lid, select Pressure Cook and cook for 24 minutes at High.

Once ready, do a quick pressure release. Remove to a cutting board and slice before serving.

Pork & Mushroom Stew

Servings: 2 | Prep + Cook Time: 50 minutes

INGREDIENTS

2 pork chops, bones removed and cut into pieces
1 cup crimini mushrooms, chopped
2 large carrots, chopped
½ tsp garlic powder
1 tsp salt

½ black pepper
2 tbsp butter
1 cup beef broth
1 tbsp apple cider vinegar
2 tbsp cornstarch

DIRECTIONS

Season the meat with salt and pepper. Add butter and pork chops to the pot and brown for 10 minutes, stirring occasionally, on Sauté mode. Add mushrooms and cook for 5 minutes. Add the remaining ingredients and seal the lid. Cook on High Pressure for 25 minutes. Do a quick release and serve hot.

Fennel Pork Estofado

Servings: 4 | Prep + Cook Time: 40 minutes

INGREDIENTS

12 oz pork neck, cut into bite-sized pieces
2 tbsp flour
1 tbsp fennel seeds, crushed
4 tbsp vegetable oil
2 onions, peeled, chopped
1 carrot

A handful of chopped celery
10 oz button mushrooms
4 cups beef broth
1 chili pepper, chopped
1 tbsp cayenne pepper

DIRECTIONS

Heat oil on Sauté. Add onions and cook for 2 minutes, until translucent. Add flour, chili pepper, carrot, celery, cayenne pepper, and fennel seeds, and continue cooking for 2 more minutes, stirring constantly.

Press Cancel, and add meat, mushrooms, beef broth, and water. Seal the lid and cook on Manual/Pressure Cook mode for 30 minutes on High Pressure. Do a quick release and serve immediately.

Honey-Mustard Pork Chops

Servings: 4 | Prep + Cook Time: 60 minutes

INGREDIENTS

2 lb pork chops
1 cup beef broth
2 tbsp oil
¼ cup honey
1 tbsp Dijon mustard

½ tsp cinnamon
1 tsp ginger, grated
1 tsp salt
½ tsp pepper, ground

DIRECTIONS

Season the chops with salt and pepper. Heat oil on Sauté and brown the chops for 2-3 minutes, on each side. In a bowl, mix honey, mustard, cinnamon, and ginger. Whisk together and drizzle over chops. Pour in broth and seal the lid. Cook on High Pressure for 30 minutes. Do a quick release and serve hot.

Jalapeño Pork

Servings: 4 | Prep + Cook Time: 60 minutes

INGREDIENTS

1 lb pork shoulder
2 tbsp olive oil
3 Jalapeño peppers, seeded and finely chopped
1 tsp ground cumin

3 cups water
1 large onion, roughly chopped
2 garlic cloves, crushed
3 cups beef broth

INSTRUCTIONS:

Heat oil on Sauté and cook the jalapeno peppers for 3 minutes. Add in all the spices, garlic and onion and stir-fry for another 2 minutes, until soft. Add in the pork shoulder, beef broth and the pureed mixture. Seal the lid, and cook on Meat/Stew for 30 minutes on High. Release the pressure quickly and serve hot.

Dinner Pork Roast

Prep + Cook Time: 45 minutes | Servings: 6

INGREDIENTS

3 pounds Sirloin Pork Roast
1 tbsp Honey
1 tsp Chili Powder
1 tbsp Rosemary

1 tbsp Olive Oil
1 ¼ cups Water
2 tbsp Lemon Juice

DIRECTIONS

Combine the spices, in a bowl, and rub them onto the pork. Heat oil on SAUTÉ mode and sear the pork on all sides. Stir in the remaining ingredients and seal the lid. Cook for 30 minutes, on MEAT/STEW at High. Do a natural pressure release, for 15 minutes.

Basil-Flavored Pork Stew

Servings: 4 | Prep + Cook Time: 45 minutes

INGREDIENTS

16 oz pork tenderloin, cut into bite-sized pieces
1 onion, peeled, chopped
2 tbsp vegetable oil
4 tomatoes, peeled, diced
½ tbsp red wine

½ tbsp beef broth
A handful of fresh basil
1 tsp salt
¼ tsp pepper

DIRECTIONS

Heat oil and stir-fry the onions, until translucent. Add the meat, salt, pepper, wine, and basil. Cook for 10 minutes. Pour in broth, seal the lid and cook on High Pressure for 25 minutes. Do a quick release.

Do a quick release. Season with salt, pepper, and red pepper flakes. Add butter and cook until the liquid evaporates – for 10 minutes, on Sauté mode.

Pork Roast with Mushrooms Sauce

Servings: 6 | Prep + Cook Time: 65 minutes

INGREDIENTS

2 lb pork shoulder
1 cup button mushrooms, chopped
2 tbsp butter, unsalted
1 tbsp balsamic vinegar
½ tsp garlic powder

1 tsp salt
¼ cup soy sauce
2 bay leaves
1 cup beef broth
2 tbsp cornstarch

DIRECTIONS

Rinse the meat and rub with salt and garlic powder. Melt butter on Sauté. Brown the meat for 5 minutes on each side. Stir in soy sauce and bay leaves.

Cook for 2 minutes before, add in beef broth and balsamic vinegar. Seal the lid and set on Meat/Stew mode. Cook for 30 minutes on High Pressure.

When done, do a quick release and stir in mushrooms. Cook until tender, about 5 minutes, on Sauté mode. Stir in cornstarch and cook for 2 minutes.

Pork Chops with Mushrooms in Tomato Sauce

Prep + Cook Time: 35 minutes | Servings: 4

INGREDIENTS

4 large bone-in pork chops
1 cup tomato sauce
1 ½ cups white button mushrooms, sliced
1 onion, chopped

1 tsp garlic, minced
½ cup water
1 tbsp oil
Salt and black pepper, to taste

DIRECTIONS

Heat oil on SAUTÉ. Add garlic, onion and cook for 2 minutes, until soft and fragrant. Add pork and cook until browned on all sides. Stir in the remaining ingredients and seal the lid.

Cook for 20 minutes on MEAT/STEW mode at High. When ready, do a quick pressure release.

Beans with Pancetta, Kale & Chickpeas

Prep + Cook Time: 30 minutes | Servings: 8

INGREDIENTS

5 cups Water, divided
1 pack (2 oz) Onion soup mix
¼ cup Olive Oil
1 tbsp Garlic, minced
1 ½ pounds canned Chickpeas, soaked overnight
2 tsp Mustard
½ pound Pancetta slices, chopped
1 Onion, chopped
1 cup Kale, chopped

DIRECTIONS

Heat the oil and cook the onions, garlic, and pancetta for 5 minutes on SAUTÉ mode. Add 1 cup of water and the soup mix, and cook for 5 more minutes. Then, add the chickpeas and 4 cups of water.

Add in the kale and mustard. Seal the lid and cook for 15 minutes on Pressure Cook at High Pressure. Once cooking is completed, perform a quick pressure release and serve immediately.

Pork Cutlets with Baby Carrots

Prep + Cook Time: 30 minutes | Servings: 4

INGREDIENTS

1 pound Pork Cutlets
1 pound Baby Carrots
1 Onion, sliced
1 tbsp Butter
1 cup Vegetable Broth
1 tsp Garlic Powder
Salt and Black Pepper, to taste

DIRECTIONS

Season the pork with salt and pepper. Melt butter on SAUTÉ, and brown the pork on all sides. Stir in carrots and onions and cook for 2 more minutes, until soft.

Pour in the broth, and add garlic powder. Season with salt and pepper. Seal the lid and cook for 20 minutes on MEAT/STEW mode at High. When ready, release the pressure quickly.

Pork Sausage with Bell Peppers & Sweet Onions

Prep + Cook Time: 20 minutes | Servings: 8

INGREDIENTS

8 Pork Sausages
2 large Sweet Onions, sliced
4 Red Bell Peppers, cut into strips
1 tbsp Olive Oil
½ cup Beef Broth
¼ cup White Wine
1 tsp Garlic, minced

DIRECTIONS

On SAUTÉ, add the sausages, and brown them for a few minutes. Remove to a plate and discard the liquid. Press CANCEL. Wipe clean the cooker and heat the oil on SAUTÉ mode.

Stir in onions and peppers. Stir-fry them for 5 minutes, until soft. Add garlic and cook for a minute. Add the sausages and pour in broth and wine. Seal the lid and cook for 5 minutes at High pressure. Once done, do a quick pressure release.

Spicy Ground Pork

Prep + Cook Time: 55 minutes | Servings: 6

INGREDIENTS

2 pounds ground pork
1 onion, diced
1 can diced tomatoes
1 can peas
5 garlic cloves, crushed
3 tbsp butter
1 serrano pepper, chopped
1 cup beef broth

1 tsp ground ginger
2 tsp ground coriander
1 tsp salt
¾ tsp cumin
¼ tsp cayenne pepper
½ tsp turmeric
½ tsp black pepper

DIRECTIONS

Melt butter on SAUTÉ mode. Add onions and cook for 3 minutes, until soft. Stir in the spices and garlic and cook for 2 more minutes. Add pork and cook until browned.

Pour broth and add serrano pepper, peas, and tomatoes. Seal the lid and cook for 30 minutes on MEAT/STEW mode at High. When ready, release the pressure naturally for 10 minutes.

Marinated Flank Steak

Prep + Cook Time: 80 minutes | Servings: 4

INGREDIENTS

2 pounds Flank Steak
1 cup Beef Broth
1 Onion, diced

Marinade:
2 tbsp Fish Sauce
½ tsp Cajun Seasoning
2 tsp Garlic, minced

2 tbsp Potato Starch
1 Carrot, chopped
Cooking Spray, to grease

½ cup Soy Sauce
1 tbsp Sesame Oil

DIRECTIONS

Combine marinade ingredients in a bowl. Add in the beef and let marinate for 30 minutes.

Coat the pressure cooker with cooking spray. Add onions and carrots and cook until soft on SAUTÉ. Add the beef along with the marinade. Whisk in the broth and starch.

Seal the lid and cook for 40 minutes on MEAT/STEW at High. Do a quick release and serve.

Sweet & Sour Pork

Servings: 4 | Prep + Cook Time: 40 minutes

INGREDIENTS

1 pound pork loin, cut into chunks
2 tbsp white wine
15 ounces canned peaches
¼ cup beef stock
2 tbsp sweet chili sauce

2 tbsp honey
2 tbsp soy sauce
2 tbsp cornstarch
¼ cup water

DIRECTIONS

Into the pot, mix soy sauce, beef stock, wine, juice from the canned peaches, and sweet chili sauce. Stir in pork to coat. Seal the lid and cook on High Pressure for 5 minutes.

Release pressure naturally for 10 minutes, then release the remaining pressure quickly. Remove the pork to a serving plate. Chop the peaches into small pieces.

In a bowl, mix water with cornstarch until well dissolved; stir the mixture into the pot. Press Sauté and cook for 5 more minutes until you obtain the desired thick consistency. Add in the chopped peaches and stir well. Serve the pork topped with peach sauce and enjoy.

Pork Fillets with Tomato Sauce

Prep + Cook Time: 30 minutes | Servings: 6

INGREDIENTS

1 lb Pork Loin Filets
16 ounces canned peach
½ tsp Black Pepper
½ tsp Cilantro, ground
½ tsp Ginger, finely chopped
½ cup Worcestershire sauce
¼ cup Apple Cider Vinegar

½ tsp Garlic, minced
1 tsp Salt
1 cup Onions, sliced
1 tbsp Brown Sugar
2 tbsp Olive Oil
1 cup Tomato Sauce
1 tbsp Arrowroot slurry

DIRECTIONS

On SAUTÉ mode, heat oil. Cook onions until tender, for about 4 minutes. Stir in the remaining ingredients, except for the arrowroot. Seal the lid, Select MEAT/STEW and cook for 20 minutes at High.

Do a quick pressure release. Stir in the arrowroot slurry and cook on SAUTÉ, until the sauce thickens.

BEEF & LAMB

Beef with Garbanzo Beans

Servings: 10 | Prep + Cook Time: 45 minutes

INGREDIENTS

1 lb garbanzo beans, soaked overnight
1 tbsp olive oil
2 onions, finely chopped
2 ½ pounds ground beef
1 small jalapeño with seeds, minced
6 garlic cloves, minced
¼ cup chili powder
2 tbsp ground cumin
2 tsp salt
1 tsp smoked paprika
1 tsp dried oregano
1 tsp garlic powder
¼ tsp cayenne pepper
2 ½ cups beef broth
1 (6-ounce) can tomato puree

DIRECTIONS

Add the beans and pour in cold water to cover 1 inch. Seal the lid and cook for 20 minutes on High Pressure. Release the pressure quickly.

Drain beans and rinse with cold water. Wipe clean the pot and set to Sauté mode. Warm olive oil and sauté onion for 3 minutes until soft. Add jalapeño, beef, and garlic, and stir-fry for 5 minutes until is cooked through.

Stir in chili powder, salt, garlic powder, paprika, cumin, oregano, and cayenne, and cook until soft, about 30 seconds. Pour in broth, beans, and tomato puree.

Seal the lid and cook for 20 minutes on High Pressure. Release the pressure naturally, for about 10 minutes.

Open the lid, press Sauté, and cook as you stir until desired consistency is attained. Spoon chili into bowls to serve.

Beef & Bacon Chili

Servings: 6 | Prep + Cook Time: 1 hour

INGREDIENTS

2 pounds stewing beef, trimmed
4 tsp salt,
4 ounces smoked bacon, cut into strips
1 tsp freshly ground black pepper
2 tsp olive oil
1 onion, diced
2 bell peppers, diced
3 garlic cloves, minced
1 tbsp ground cumin
1 tsp chili powder
½ tsp cayenne pepper
1 chipotle in adobo sauce, finely chopped
2 cups beef broth
29 ounces canned whole tomatoes
15 ounces canned kidney beans, drained

DIRECTIONS

Set on Sauté mode and fry the bacon until crispy, about 5 minutes. Set aside.

Rub the beef with ½ teaspoon black pepper and 1 teaspoon salt. In the bacon fat, brown beef for 5-6 minutes; Transfer to a plate. Warm the oil. Add in garlic, peppers and onion and sauté for 3 to 4 minutes until soft. Stir in cumin, cayenne pepper, the extra pepper, salt, chipotle, chili powder and cook for 30 seconds until soft.

Return beef and bacon to the pot with vegetables and spices; add in tomatoes and broth. Seal the lid and cook on High Pressure for 45 minutes. Release the Pressure quickly. Stir in beans. Let simmer on Keep Warm for 10 minutes until flavors combine.

Brisket Chili con Carne

Servings: 6 | Prep + Cook Time: 1 hour 25 minutes

INGREDIENTS

1 tbsp ground black pepper
2 tsp salt
1 tsp sweet paprika
1 tsp cayenne pepper
1 tsp chili powder
½ tsp garlic salt
14 ounces canned black beans, drained and rinsed
½ tsp onion powder
1 (4 pounds) beef brisket
1 cup beef broth
2 bay leaves
2 tbsp Worcestershire sauce

DIRECTIONS

In a bowl, combine pepper, paprika, chili powder, cayenne pepper, salt, onion powder and garlic salt; rub onto brisket pieces to coat.

Add the brisket to your instant pot. Cover with Worcestershire sauce and water.

Seal the lid and cook on High Pressure for 50 minutes. Release the pressure naturally for 10 minutes.

Transfer the brisket to a cutting board. Drain any liquid present in the pot using a fine-mesh strainer; get rid of any solids and fat.

Slice brisket, arrange the slices onto a platter, add the black beans on side and spoon the cooking liquid over the slices and beans to serve.

Beef Stew with Veggies

Servings: 6 | Prep + Cook Time: 1 hour 15 minutes

INGREDIENTS

¼ cup flour
2 tsp salt
1 tsp paprika
1 tsp ground black pepper
2 pounds beef chuck, cubed
2 tbsp olive oil
2 tbsp butter
1 onion, diced
3 garlic cloves, minced
1 cup dry red wine
2 cups beef stock
1 tbsp dried Italian Seasoning
2 tsp Worcestershire sauce
4 cups potatoes, diced
2 celery stalks, chopped
3 cups carrots, chopped
3 tomatoes, chopped
2 bell peppers, thinly chopped
Salt and ground black pepper to taste
A handful of fresh parsley, chopped

DIRECTIONS

In a bowl, mix black pepper, beef, flour, paprika, and 1 teaspoon salt. Toss the ingredients and ensure the beef is well-coated. Warm butter and oil on Sauté mode. Add in beef and cook for 8-10 minutes until browned. Set aside.

To the same fat, add garlic, onion, and celery, bell peppers, and cook for 4-5 minutes until tender.

Deglaze with wine, scrape the bottom to get rid of any browned beef bits. Pour in remaining salt, beef stock, Worcestershire sauce, and Italian seasoning.

Return beef to the pot; add carrots, tomatoes, and potatoes. Seal the lid, press Meat/Stew and cook on High Pressure for 35 minutes. Release Pressure naturally for 10 minutes. Taste and adjust the seasonings as necessary. Serve on plates and scatter over the parsley.

Beef and Pumpkin Stew

Servings: 6 | Prep + Cook Time: 35 minutes

INGREDIENTS

2 tbsp canola oil
2 pounds stew beef, cut into 1-inch chunks
1 cup red wine
1 onion, chopped
1 tsp garlic powder
1 tsp salt

3 whole cloves
1 bay leaf
3 carrots, chopped
½ butternut pumpkin, chopped
2 tbsp cornstarch
3 tbsp water

DIRECTIONS

Warm oil on Sauté mode. Brown the beef for 5 minutes on each side.

Deglaze the pot with wine, scrape the bottom to get rid of any browned beef bits. Add in onion, salt, bay leaf, cloves, and garlic powder. Seal the lid, press Meat/Stew and cook on High for 15 minutes.

Release the Pressure quickly. Add in pumpkin and carrots without stirring.

Seal the lid and cook on High Pressure for 5 minutes. Release the Pressure quickly.

In a bowl, mix water and cornstarch until cornstarch dissolves completely; mix into the stew. Allow the stew to simmer while uncovered on Keep Warm for 5 minutes until you attain the desired thickness.

Greek Beef Gyros

Servings: 4 | Prep + Cook Time: 55 minutes

INGREDIENTS

1 pound beef sirloin, cut into thin strips
1 onion, thinly chopped
⅓ cup beef broth
2 tbsp fresh lemon juice
2 tbsp olive oil
2 tsp dry oregano

1 clove garlic, minced
Salt and ground black pepper to taste
4 slices pita bread
1 cup Greek yogurt
2 tbsp fresh dill, chopped

DIRECTIONS

In the pot, mix beef, beef broth, oregano, garlic, lemon juice, pepper, onion, olive oil, and salt.

Seal the lid and cook on High Pressure for 30 minutes. Release Pressure naturally for 15 minutes, then turn steam vent valve to Venting to release the remaining Pressure quickly.

Divide the beef mixture between the pita breads, Top with yogurt and dill, and roll up to serve.

Beef Stew with Eggplant & Parmesan

Servings: 6 | Prep + Cook Time: 50 minutes

INGREDIENTS

9 oz beef neck, cut into bite-sized pieces
1 eggplant, chopped
2 cups fire-roasted tomatoes
½ tbsp fresh green peas
1 tbsp beef broth

4 tbsp olive oil
2 tbsp tomato paste
1 tbsp ground chili pepper
½ tsp kosher salt
Parmesan cheese, for garnish

DIRECTIONS

Rub the meat with salt, cayenne, and chili pepper. Grease the instant pot with oil and brown the meat for 5-7 minutes, or until golden, on Sauté mode.

Add all the remaining ingredients and seal the lid. Cook on Meat/Stew mode for 40 minutes on High. Do a natural release, for 10 minutes. Serve warm, sprinkled with freshly grated Parmesan Cheese.

Meatloaf & Cheesy Mashed Potatoes

Servings: 6 | Prep + Cook Time: 45 minutes

INGREDIENTS

Meatloaf:
1 ½ pounds ground beef
1 onion, diced
1 egg
1 potato, grated

¼ cup tomato puree
1 tsp garlic powder
1 tsp salt
1 tsp ground black pepper

Mashed Potatoes:
4 potatoes, chopped
2 cups water
½ cup milk
2 tbsp butter

1 tsp salt
½ tsp ground black pepper
1 cup ricotta cheese

DIRECTIONS

In a bowl, combine ground beef, eggs, 1 tsp pepper, garlic powder, potato, onion, tomato puree, and 1 tsp salt to obtain a consistent texture. Shape the mixture into a meatloaf and place onto an aluminum foil.

Arrange potatoes in the pot and pour water over them. Place a trivet onto the potatoes and set the foil sheet with meatloaf onto trivet. Seal the lid and cook on High Pressure for 22 minutes. Release the Pressure quickly.

Take the meatloaf from the pot and set on a cutting board to cool before slicing. Drain the liquid out of the pot. Mash potatoes in the pot with ½ teaspoon pepper, milk, ricotta cheese, 1 teaspoon salt, and butter until smooth and all the liquid is absorbed.

Divide potatoes into serving plates and lean a meatloaf slice to one side of the potato pile before serving.

Beef & Vegetable Stew

Servings: 6 | Prep + Cook Time: 35 minutes

INGREDIENTS

2 lb beef meat for stew
¾ cup red wine
1 tbsp ghee
6 oz tomato paste
6 oz baby carrots, chopped
2 sweet potatoes, cut into chunks

1 onion, finely chopped
½ tsp salt
4 cups beef broth
½ cup green peas
1 tsp dried thyme
3 garlic cloves, crushed

INSTRUCTIONS:

Heat the ghee on Sauté. Add beef and brown for 5-6 minutes. Add onions and garlic, and keep stirring for 3 more minutes. Add the remaining ingredients and seal the lid. Cook on Meat/Stew for 20 minutes on High pressure. Do a quick release and serve immediately.

Italian-Style Pot Roast

Servings: 5 | Prep + Cook Time: 1 hour 30 minutes

INGREDIENTS

2 ½ pounds beef brisket, trimmed
Salt and freshly ground black pepper
2 tbsp olive oil
1 onion, chopped
3 garlic cloves, minced
1 cup beef broth
¾ cup dry red wine

2 fresh thyme sprigs
2 fresh rosemary sprigs
4 ounces pancetta, chopped
6 carrots, chopped
1 bay leaf
A handful of parsley, chopped

DIRECTIONS

Warm oil on Sauté. Fry the pancetta for 4-5 minutes until crispy. Set aside. Season the beef with pepper and salt, and brown for 5 to 7 minutes per each. Remove and set aside on a plate.

In the same oil, fry garlic and onion for 3 minutes until soften. Pour in red wine and beef broth to deglaze the bottom, scrape the bottom of the pot to get rid of any browned bits of food.

Return the beef and pancetta to the pot and add rosemary sprigs and thyme.

Seal the lid and cook for 50 minutes on High Pressure. Release the Pressure quickly. Add carrots and bay leaf to the pot. Seal the lid and cook for an additional 4 minutes on High Pressure.

Release the Pressure quickly. Get rid of the thyme, bay leaf and rosemary sprigs. Place beef on a serving plate and sprinkle with parsley to serve.

Meatballs with Marinara Sauce

Servings: 6 | Prep + Cook Time: 35 minutes

INGREDIENTS

1½ pounds ground beef
⅓ cup warm water
¾ cup grated Parmigiano-Reggiano cheese
½ cup bread crumbs
1 egg
2 tbsp fresh parsley

¼ tsp garlic powder
¼ tsp dried oregano
Salt and ground black pepper to taste
½ cup capers
1 tsp olive oil
3 cups marinara sauce

DIRECTIONS

In a bowl, mix ground beef, garlic powder, pepper, oregano, crumbs, egg, and salt; shape into meatballs. Warm oil on Sauté mode. Add meatballs to the oil and brown for 2-3 minutes and all sides.

Pour water and marinara sauce over the meatballs. Seal the lid and cook on High Pressure for 10 minutes. Release the Pressure quickly. Serve in large bowls topped with capers and Parmigiano-Reggiano cheese.

Crispy Beef with Rice

Servings: 4 | Prep + Cook Time: 55 minutes

INGREDIENTS

2 lb beef shoulder
1 cup rice
2 cups beef broth

3 tbsp butter
1 tsp salt
½ tsp pepper

DIRECTIONS

Rinse the meat and rub with salt. Place it in the pot and pour in broth. Seal the lid and cook on Meat/Stew for 25 minutes on High Pressure. Do a quick release, remove the meat but keep the broth.

Add rice and stir in 1 tbsp of butter. Seal the lid, and cook on Rice mode for 8 minutes on High. Do a quick release. Remove the rice and wipe the pot clean. Melt 2 tbsp of butter on Sauté.

Add meat and lightly brown for 10 minutes. Serve with rice and season with pepper and salt.

Short Ribs with Mushroom & Asparagus Sauce

Servings: 6 | Prep + Cook Time: 1 hour 15 minutes

INGREDIENTS

3½ pounds boneless beef short ribs, cut into pieces
2 tsp salt
1 tsp ground black pepper
3 tbsp olive oil
1 onion, diced
1 cup dry red wine
1 tbsp tomato puree
2 carrots, peeled and chopped
2 garlic cloves, minced

5 sprigs parsley, chopped
2 sprigs rosemary, chopped
3 sprigs oregano, chopped
4 cups beef stock
10 ounces mushrooms, quartered
1 cup asparagus, trimmed chopped
1 tbsp cornstarch
¼ cup cold water

DIRECTIONS

Season the ribs with black pepper and salt. Warm oil on Sauté. In batches, add the short ribs to the oil and cook for 3 to 5 minutes each side until browned. Set aside. Add onions and sauté for 4 minutes until soft.

Add tomato puree and red wine into the pot to deglaze, scrape the bottom to get rid of any browned beef bits. Cook for 2 minutes until wine reduces slightly.

Return the ribs to the pot and top with carrots, oregano, rosemary, and garlic. Add in broth and press Cancel.

Seal the lid, press Meat/Stew and cook on High for 35 minutes. Release Pressure naturally for 10 minutes. Transfer ribs to a plate. Strain and get rid of herbs and vegetables, and return cooking broth to inner pot. Add mushrooms and asparagus to the broth. Press Sauté and cook for 2 to 4 minutes until soft.

In a bowl, mix water and cornstarch until cornstarch dissolves completely. Add the cornstarch mixture into broth as you stir for 1 to 3 minutes until the broth thickens slightly. Season the sauce with black pepper and salt. Pour the sauce over ribs, add chopped parsley for garnish before serving.

Beef & Mushroom Steaks

Servings: 4 | Prep + Cook Time: 35 minutes

INGREDIENTS

1 lb beef steaks
1 lb button mushrooms, thinly chopped
2 tbsp vegetable oil
1 tsp salt

½ tsp freshly ground black pepper
1 bay leaf
1 tbsp dried thyme
6 oz cherry tomatoes

DIRECTIONS

Rub steaks with salt, pepper, and thyme. Place in the instant pot. Pour in 3 cups of water, add bay leaf and seal the lid. Cook on High pressure for 13 minutes. Do a quick release and set the steaks aside. Heat oil on Sauté, and stir-fry mushrooms and tomatoes for 5 minutes. Add steaks and brown on both sides.

Beef Stew with Green Peas

Servings: 4 | Prep + Cook Time: 15 minutes

INGREDIENTS

2 lb beef, tender cuts, boneless, cut into bits
2 cups green peas
1 onion, diced
1 tomato, diced
3 cups beef broth
½ cup tomato paste
1 tsp cayenne pepper, ground
1 tbsp flour
1 tsp salt
½ tsp dried thyme, ground
½ tsp red pepper flakes

DIRECTIONS

Add all ingredients in the instant pot. Seal the lid, press Manual/Pressure Cook and cook for 10 minutes on High Pressure. When done, release the steam naturally, for 10 minutes and serve.

Italian Beef Sandwiches with Pesto

Servings: 4 | Prep + Cook Time: 1 hour

INGREDIENTS

1 ½ pounds beef steak, cut into strips
Salt and ground black pepper
1 tbsp olive oil
¼ cup dry red wine
1 cup beef broth
1 tbsp oregano
1 tsp onion powder
1 tsp garlic powder
4 hoagie rolls, halved
8 slices mozzarella cheese
½ cup pepperoncini peppers
4 tbsp pesto

DIRECTIONS

Season the beef cubes with salt and pepper. Warm oil on Sauté and sear the beef for 2 to 3 minutes for each side until browned. Add wine into the pot to deglaze, scrape the bottom to get rid of any browned beef bits. Stir garlic powder, beef broth, onion powder, and oregano into the pot.

Seal the lid, press Meat/Stew and cook for 25 minutes on High. Release Pressure naturally for 10 minutes. Spread each bread half with pesto, put beef on top, place pepperoncini slices over, add mozzarella cheese slices and cover with the second half of bread to serve.

Italian-Style Calf's Liver

Servings: 2 | Prep + Cook Time: 10 minutes

INGREDIENTS

1 lb calf's liver, rinsed
3 tbsp olive oil
2 garlic cloves, crushed
1 tbsp fresh mint, finely chopped
½ tbsp cayenne pepper
1 tsp salt
½ tsp Italian Seasoning

DIRECTIONS

In a bowl, mix oil, garlic, mint, cayenne, salt and Italian seasoning. Brush the liver and chill for 30 minutes. Remove from the fridge and pat dry with paper.

Place the liver into the inner pot. Seal the lid and cook on High Pressure for 5 minutes. When ready, release the steam naturally, for about 10 minutes.

Rosemary Meatloaf

Servings: 6 | Prep + Cook Time: 60 minutes

INGREDIENTS

2 lb ground beef
2 large eggs
½ tsp minced garlic
1 cup all-purpose flour

1 tsp dried thyme, ground
3 tbsp olive oil
1 tsp dried rosemary, ground
½ tsp salt

DIRECTIONS

In a bowl, combine the meat, flour, and eggs. Sprinkle with thyme, rosemary and salt. Mix with hands until well incorporated, and set aside.

Grease a baking dish with olive oil. Form the meatloaf at the bottom. Add 1 ½ cups of water and place a trivet in your cooker. Lay the baking dish on the trivet. Seal the lid, Press Meat/Stew and cook for 40 minutes on High.

Do a quick release. Carefully transfer the meatloaf to a serving dish. Garnish with vegetable salad or mashed potatoes, to serve.

Peppery Beef

Servings: 6 | Prep + Cook Time: 45 minutes

INGREDIENTS

2 lb lean beef, cut into bite-sized pieces
5 onions, peeled, chopped
5 garlic cloves, peeled, crushed
1 tsp salt
1 jalapeno pepper, deveined and chopped

1 bell pepper, deveined and chopped
Freshly ground black pepper, to taste
1 tsp cayenne pepper
2 tbsp tomato sauce
2 tbsp vegetable oil

DIRECTIONS

Heat oil on Sauté. Stir-fry onions, garlic, for 2-3 minutes. Add the meat, salt, pepper, cayenne pepper, and tomato sauce. Mix well and pour enough water to cover. Seal the lid and cook for 20 minutes on High Pressure. Do a quick pressure release.

Lemony Lamb Stew

Servings: 4 | Prep + Cook Time: 60 minutes

INGREDIENTS

1 lb lamb neck, boneless
2 potatoes, peeled, cut into bite-sized pieces
2 large carrots, chopped
1 tomato, diced
1 small red bell pepper, chopped

1 garlic head, whole
A handful of parsley, chopped
¼ cup lemon juice
½ tsp salt
½ tsp black pepper, ground

DIRECTIONS

Add the meat and season with salt. Add in the remaining ingredients, tuck in one garlic head in the middle of the pot and add 2 cups of water. Add a handful of fresh parsley and seal the lid.

Cook on High Pressure for 45 minutes. When ready, do a quick release.

Beef & Eggplant Casserole

Servings: 2 | Prep + Cook Time: 35 minutes

INGREDIENTS

2 eggplants, peeled, cut lengthwise
1 cup lean ground beef
1 onion, chopped
1 tsp olive oil
¼ tsp. freshly ground black pepper
2 tomatoes
3 tbsp freshly chopped parsley

DIRECTIONS

Place eggplants in a bowl and season with salt. Let sit for 10 minutes. Rinse well and drain. Grease the inner pot with oil. Stir-fry onions for 2 minutes, until soft.

Add ground beef, tomato, and cook for 5 minutes. Remove from the pot and transfer to a deep bowl. Make a layer with eggplant slices in the pot.

Spread the ground beef mixture over and sprinkle with parsley. Make another layer with eggplants and repeat until you've used up all ingredients.

Seal the lid and cook on High Pressure for 12 minutes. Do a quick release.

Beef Stuffed Red Peppers

Servings: 4 | Prep + Cook Time: 35 minutes

INGREDIENTS

2 lb red bell peppers, stems and seed removed
1 onion, finely chopped
1 lb lean ground beef
¼ cup rice
½ cup tomatoes
1 tomato, chopped
½ tsp salt
1 tsp cayenne pepper
3 tbsp olive oil

DIRECTIONS

In a bowl, combine meat, onion, rice, tomatoes, salt, and cayenne. Stir well to combine. Use 2 tbsp of this mixture and fill each pepper.

Make sure to leave at least ½ inch of headspace. Grease the bottom of your instant pot with cooking spray. Make the first layer with tomato slices.

Arrange the peppers and add two cups of water. Seal the lid, and cook on High Pressure for 15 minutes. Do a natural Pressure release, for 10 minutes.

Beef & Rice Stuffed Onions

Servings: 4 | Prep + Cook Time: 30 minutes

INGREDIENTS

10 sweet onions, peeled
1 lb of lean ground beef
½ tbsp rice
3 tbsp olive oil
1 tbsp dry mint, ground
1 tsp cayenne pepper, ground
½ tsp cumin, ground
1 tsp salt
½ tbsp tomato paste
½ cup bread crumbs
A handful of fresh parsley, finely chopped

DIRECTIONS

Cut a ¼-inch slice from top of each onion and trim a small amount from the bottom end, this will make the onions stand upright. Place onions in a microwave-safe dish, and pour one cup of water.

Cover with a tight lid and microwave for 10-12 minutes or until onions soften. Remove onions and cool slightly. Carefully remove inner layers of onions with a paring knife, leaving about a ¼-inch onion shell.

In a bowl, combine beef, rice, oil, mint, cayenne pepper, cumin, salt, and bread crumbs. Use one tablespoon of the mixture to fill the onions. Grease the inner pot with oil. Add onions and pour 2.5 cups of water.

Seal the lid and cook on Manual/Pressure Cook for 10 minutes on High. Do a quick release. Top with parsley and serve with sour cream and pide bread.

Sour Potato Beef Lasagne

Servings: 4 | Prep + Cook Time: 30 minutes

INGREDIENTS

2 lb potatoes, peeled, chopped
1 lb lean ground beef
1 onion, peeled, chopped
1 tsp salt
½ tsp freshly ground black pepper
½ cup milk
2 eggs, beaten
Vegetable oil
Sour cream for serving

DIRECTIONS

Grease the bottom of the pot with oil. Make one layer of potatoes and brush with milk. Spread the ground beef on top and make another layer of potatoes.

Brush well with the remaining milk, 2 cups. Seal the lid, and cook for 15 minutes on High Pressure. When ready, do a quick release.

Open the lid, and make the final layer with the beaten eggs. Seal the lid and let it stand for about 10 minutes. Top with sour cream to serve.

Eggplant Stew with Almonds

Servings: 4 | Prep + Cook Time: 30 minutes

INGREDIENTS

3 eggplants, halved
2 tomatoes, chopped
2 red bell peppers, chopped, seeds removed
¼ tbsp tomato paste
1 bunch of fresh parsley, chopped
3 oz toasted almonds, chopped
2 tbsp salted capers, rinsed, drained
¼ cup extra virgin olive oil
1 tsp sea salt

DIRECTIONS

Grease the instant pot with 2 tbsp of olive oil. Make the first layer with halved eggplants tucking the ends Gently to fit in.

Make the second layer with tomatoes and red bell peppers. Spread the tomato paste evenly over the vegetables, sprinkle with almonds and salted capers.

Add the remaining olive oil, salt and pepper. Pour 1 ½ cups of water and seal the lid. Cook on High Pressure for 13 minutes. Do a quick release.

Classic Italian Lamb Ragout

Servings: 6 | Prep + Cook Time: 25 minutes

INGREDIENTS

1 lb lamb chops, 1-inch thick
1 cup water
1 cup green peas, rinsed
3 carrots, peeled, chopped
3 onions, peeled, chopped

1 potato, peeled, chopped
1 tomato, peeled, roughly chopped
3 tbsp olive oil
1 tbsp paprika
Salt and black pepper to taste

DIRECTIONS

Grease the instant pot with olive oil. Rub salt onto meat and make a bottom layer. Add peas, carrots, onions, potatoes, and tomato. Season with paprika.

Add olive oil, water, salt, and pepper. Give it a good stir and seal the lid. Cook on Meat/Stew mode for 20 minutes on High Pressure. When ready, do a natural Pressure release, for about 10 minutes.

Garlic & Pancetta Lamb Leg

Servings: 6 | Prep + Cook Time: 60 minutes

INGREDIENTS

2 lb lamb leg
6 garlic cloves
1 large onion, chopped
6 pancetta slices
1 tsp rosemary

½ tsp salt
¼ tsp freshly ground black pepper
2 tbsp oil
3 cups beef broth

INSTRUCTIONS:

Heat oil on Sauté. Add pancetta and onions, making two layers. Season with salt and cook for 3 minutes, until browned. Meanwhile, place the meat in a separate dish.

Using a sharp knife, make 6 incisions into the meat and place a garlic clove in each. Rub the meat with spices and transfer to the pot. Press Cancel and pour in beef broth. Seal the lid and cook on High pressure for 25 minutes. When done, do a natural pressure release, for about 10 minutes.

Sesame Lamb

Servings: 4 | Prep + Cook Time: 40 minutes

INGREDIENTS

1 cup rice
1 cup green peas
12 oz lamb, tender cuts, ½-inch thick
3 tbsp sesame seeds
4 cups beef broth

1 tsp sea salt
1 bay leaf
½ tsp dried thyme
3 tbsp butter

DIRECTIONS

Place the meat in the pot and pour in broth. Seal the lid and cook on High Pressure for 13 minutes. Do a quick release. Remove the meat but keep the liquid. Add rice and green peas.

Season with salt, bay leaf, and thyme. Stir well and top with the meat. Seal the lid and cook on Rice for 8 minutes on High. Do a quick release and stir in butter and sesame seeds. Serve immediately.

FISH & SEAFOOD

Steamed Mediterranean Cod

Servings: 4 | Prep + Cook Time: 20 minutes

INGREDIENTS

1 pound cherry tomatoes, halved
1 bunch fresh thyme sprigs
4 fillets cod
1 tsp olive oil
1 clove garlic, pressed
3 pinches salt

2 cups water
1 cup white rice
1 cup Kalamata olives
2 tbsp pickled capers
1 tbsp olive oil
1 pinch ground black pepper

DIRECTIONS

Line a parchment paper on the basket of your instant pot. Place about half the tomatoes in a single layer on the paper. Sprinkle with thyme, reserving some for garnish.

Arrange cod fillets on top. Sprinkle with a little bit of olive oil.

Spread the garlic, pepper, salt, and remaining tomatoes over the fish. In the pot, mix rice and water.

Lay a trivet over the rice and water. Lower steamer basket onto the trivet.

Seal the lid, and cook for 7 minutes on Low Pressure. Release the Pressure quickly.

Remove the steamer basket and trivet from the pot. Use a fork to fluff rice.

Plate the fish fillets and apply a garnish of olives, reserved thyme, pepper, remaining olive oil, and capers. Serve with rice.

Steamed Sea Bass with Turnips

Servings: 4 | Prep + Cook Time: 15 minutes

INGREDIENTS

1½ cups water
1 lemon, sliced
4 sea bass fillets
4 sprigs thyme
1 white onion, cut into thin rings

2 turnips, chopped
2 pinches salt
1 pinch ground black pepper
2 tsp olive oil

DIRECTIONS

Add water and set a rack into the pot.

Line a parchment paper to the bottom of the steamer basket. Place lemon slices in a single layer on the rack.

Arrange fillets on the top of the lemons, cover with onion and thyme sprigs. Top with turnip slices.

Drizzle pepper, salt, and olive oil over the mixture. Put steamer basket onto the rack.

Seal lid and cook on Low pressure for 8 minutes. Release the pressure quickly.

Serve over the delicate onion rings and thinly turnips.

Salmon with Dill Chutney

Servings: 2 | Prep + Cook Time: 15 minutes

INGREDIENTS

2 salmon fillets
Juice from ½ lemon
¼ tsp paprika

For Chutney:
¼ cup fresh dill
Juice from ½ lemon

Salt and freshly ground pepper to taste
2 cups water

Sea salt to taste
¼ cup extra virgin olive oil

DIRECTIONS

In a food processor, blend all the chutney ingredients until creamy. Set aside.

To your cooker, add the water and place a steamer basket.

Arrange salmon fillets skin-side down on the steamer basket. Drizzle lemon juice over salmon and sprinkle with paprika. Seal the lid and cook for 3 minutes on High Pressure. Release the pressure quickly.

Season the fillets with pepper and salt, Transfer to a serving plate and top with the dill chutney.

Spanish Chorizo & Shrimp Boil

Servings: 4 | Prep + Cook Time: 30 minutes

INGREDIENTS

3 red potatoes
3 ears corn, cut into rounds
2 cups water
1 cup white wine
4 Spanish chorizo, sliced

1 pound shrimp, peeled and deveined
2 tbsp seafood seasoning
Salt to taste
1 lemon, cut into wedges
¼ cup butter, melted

DIRECTIONS

Add all ingredients, except butter and lemon wedges. Do not stir.

Seal the lid and cook for 2 minutes on High Pressure. Release the pressure quickly.

Drain the mixture through a colander. Transfer to a serving platter. Serve with melted butter and lemon wedges.

Cod in Lemon-Sweet Sauce

Servings: 3 | Prep + Cook Time: 20 minutes

INGREDIENTS

1 lb cod fillets, skinless and boneless
1 cup maple syrup
½ cup soy sauce
3 garlic cloves, finely chopped

1 lemon, juiced
1 tsp black pepper, ground
1 tsp sea salt
1 tbsp butter

DIRECTIONS

In a bowl, mix maple syrup, soy sauce, garlic, lemon juice, pepper, and salt. Stir until combined and set aside. Grease the pot with butter. Place the fillets at the bottom and pour over the maple sauce.

Seal the lid and cook on Steam for 8 minutes on High. Release the pressure naturally, for about 5 minutes.

Spicy Tangy Salmon with Rice

Servings: 4 | Prep + Cook Time: 20 minutes

INGREDIENTS

1 cup rice
2 cups vegetable stock
4 skinless salmon fillets
1 cup green peas
3 tbsp olive oil
1 tsp salt
1 tsp freshly ground black pepper

2 limes, juiced
2 tbsp honey
1 tsp sweet paprika
2 jalapeño peppers, seeded and diced
4 garlic cloves, minced
½ cup canned corn kernels, drained
2 tbsp chopped fresh dill

DIRECTIONS

Add in rice, stock, and salt. Place a trivet over the rice. In a bowl, mix oil, lime juice, honey, paprika, jalapeño, garlic, and dill. Coat the fish with the honey sauce while reserving a little for garnishing.

Lay the salmon fillets on the trivet. Seal the lid and cook on High Pressure for 8 minutes. Do a quick release. Fluff the rice with a fork and mix in the green peas and corn kernels. Transfer to a serving plate and top with the salmon. Drizzle with the remaining honey sauce and enjoy.

Shrimp with Brussels Sprouts

Servings: 8 | Prep + Cook Time: 45 minutes

INGREDIENTS

1 lb large shrimp, cleaned, rinsed
6 oz Brussels sprouts, outer leaves removed
4 oz of okra, whole
2 carrots, chopped
2 cups chicken broth
2 tomatoes, diced
2 tbsp tomato paste
½ tsp cayenne pepper, ground

¼ tsp black pepper, freshly ground
1 tsp sea salt
1 cup olive oil, plus 2 tbsp
¼ cup balsamic vinegar
1 tbsp fresh rosemary, chopped
1 small celery stalk, for decoration
2 tbsp sour cream, optionally

DIRECTIONS

Mix oil, vinegar, rosemary, salt, and pepper in a large bowl. Stir and submerge the shrimp into the mixture. Toss well to coat and refrigerate for 20 minutes. Add tomatoes, paste, 2 tbsp olive oil, and cayenne pepper.

Cook on Sauté for 5 minutes, stirring constantly. Remove to a bowl, cover and set aside. Pour in broth, and add Brussels sprouts, carrots, and okra. Sprinkle with salt, black pepper and seal the lid.

Cook on High pressure for 15 minutes. Then, do a quick release. Remove the vegetables and add shrimp in the remaining broth. Seal the lid again and cook on Steam for 3 minutes on High.

Do a quick release and set aside. Add the remaining oil, and cooked vegetables. Cook for 2-3 minutes, stirring constantly, on Sauté. Remove to a bowl. Top with sour cream and drizzle with shrimp marinade.

White Wine Mussels

Servings: 5 | Prep + Cook Time: 15 minutes

INGREDIENTS

1 cup white wine
½ cup water
1 tsp garlic powder

2 pounds mussels, cleaned and debearded
Juice from 1 lemon

DIRECTIONS

In the pot, mix garlic powder, water and wine. Put the mussels into the steamer basket, rounded-side should be placed facing upwards to fit as many as possible.

Insert rack into the cooker and lower steamer basket onto the rack. Seal the lid and cook on Low Pressure for 1 minute. Release the pressure quickly.

Remove unopened mussels. Coat the mussels with the wine mixture. Serve sprinkled with lemon juice with a side of French fries or slices of toasted bread.

Paella Señorito

Servings: 5 | Prep + Cook Time: 25 minutes

INGREDIENTS

¼ cup olive oil
1 onion, chopped
1 red bell pepper, diced
2 garlic cloves, minced
1 tsp paprika
1 tsp turmeric
Salt and ground white pepper to taste

1 cup bomba rice
¼ cup frozen green peas
2 cups fish broth
1 pound frozen shrimp, peeled and deveined
Chopped fresh parsley
1 lemon, cut into wedges

DIRECTIONS

Warm oil on Sauté mode. Add in bell pepper and onions, and cook for 5 minutes until fragrant. Mix in garlic and cook for one more minute until soft.

Add paprika, pepper, salt and turmeric to the vegetables with paprika and cook for 1 minute.

Stir in fish broth and rice. Add shrimp to the rice mixture. Seal the lid and cook on High Pressure for 5 minutes.

Release the pressure quickly. Stir in green peas and let sit for 5 minutes until green peas are heated through. Serve warm garnished with parsley and lemon wedges.

Buttery Herb Trout with Green Beans

Servings: 4 | Prep + Cook Time: 20 minutes

INGREDIENTS

1 cup farro
2 cups water
4 skinless trout fillets
8 ounces green beans
1 tbsp olive oil
1 tsp freshly ground black pepper
1 tsp salt

4 tbsp melted butter
½ tbsp sugar
½ tbsp freshly squeezed lemon juice
½ tsp dried rosemary
2 garlic cloves, minced
½ tsp dried thyme

DIRECTIONS

Pour the farro and water in the pot and mix. Season with salt. In a bowl, toss the green beans with olive oil, ½ tsp of black pepper, and ½ tsp of salt. In another bowl, mix together the remaining ½ tsp of black pepper and salt, butter, sugar, lemon juice, rosemary, garlic, and rosemary.

Coat the trout with the buttery herb sauce. Insert a trivet in the pot and lay the trout fillets on the trivet. Seal the lid and cook on High Pressure for 12 minutes. Do a quick release and serve immediately.

Cod on Millet

Servings: 4 | Prep + Cook Time: 20 minutes

INGREDIENTS

1 tbsp olive oil
1 cup millet
1 yellow bell pepper, diced
1 red bell pepper, diced
2 cups chicken broth

1 cup breadcrumbs
4 tbsp melted butter
¼ cup minced fresh cilantro
1 tsp salt
4 cod fillets

DIRECTIONS

Combine oil, millet, yellow and red bell peppers in the pot, and cook for 1 minute on Sauté. Mix in the chicken broth. Place a trivet atop. In a bowl, mix crumbs, butter, cilantro, lemon zest, juice, and salt.

Spoon the breadcrumb mixture evenly on the cod fillet. Lay the fish on the trivet. Seal the lid and cook on High for 6 minutes. Do a quick release and serve immediately.

Potato Chowder with Hot Shrimp

Servings: 4 | Prep + Cook Time: 20 minutes

INGREDIENTS

4 slices pancetta, chopped
4 tbsp minced garlic
1 onion, chopped
2 potatoes, chopped
16 ounces canned corn kernels
4 cups vegetable stock
1 tsp dried rosemary

1 tsp salt
1 tsp black pepper
1 pound jumbo shrimp, peeled, deveined
1 tbsp olive oil
½ tsp red chili flakes
¾ cup heavy cream

DIRECTIONS

Fry the pancetta for 5 minutes until crispy, on Sauté mode, and set aside. Add in 2 tbsp of garlic and onion, and stir-fry for 3 minutes. Add in potatoes, corn, stock, rosemary, half of the salt, and pepper.

Seal the lid and cook on High Pressure for 10 minutes. Do a quick Pressure release. Remove to a serving bowl. In a bowl, toss the shrimp in the remaining garlic, salt, black pepper, olive oil, and flakes.

Wipe the pot clean and fry shrimp for 3-4 minutes per side, until pink. Mix in the heavy cream and cook for 2 minutes. Add shrimp to chowder, garnish with the reserved pancetta and serve immediately.

Prawn & Clam Paella

Servings: 4 | Prep + Cook Time: 30 minutes

INGREDIENTS

- 2 tbsp olive oil
- 1 onion, chopped
- 4 garlic cloves, minced
- ½ cup dry white wine
- 2 cups bomba (Spanish) rice
- 4 cups chicken stock
- 1 ½ tsp sweet paprika
- 1 tsp turmeric powder
- ½ tsp freshly ground black pepper
- ½ tsp salt
- 1 pound small clams, scrubbed
- 1 pound fresh prawns, peeled and deveined
- 1 red bell pepper, diced
- 1 lemon, cut in wedges

DIRECTIONS

Stir-fry onion and garlic in a tbsp. of oil on Sauté mode for 3 minutes. Pour in wine to deglaze, scraping the bottom of the pot of any brown. Cook for 2 minutes, until the wine is reduced by half.

Add in rice and water. Season with the paprika, turmeric, salt, and pepper. Seal the lid and cook on High Pressure for 10 minutes. Do a quick release. Remove to a plate and wipe the pot clean.

Heat the remaining oil on Sauté. Cook clams and prawns for 6 minutes, until the clams have opened and the shrimp are pink. Discard unopened clams. Arrange seafood and lemon wedges over paella, to serve.

Haddock Fillets with Crushed Potatoes

Servings: 4 | Prep + Cook Time: 25 minutes

INGREDIENTS

- 8 ounces beer
- 2 eggs
- 1 cup flour
- ½ tbsp cayenne powder
- 1 tbsp cumin powder
- Salt and pepper to taste
- 4 haddock fillets
- Nonstick cooking spray
- 4 potatoes, cut into ¼- to ½-inch matchsticks
- 2 tbsp olive oil

DIRECTIONS

In a bowl, whisk beer and eggs. In another bowl, combine flour, cayenne, cumin, black pepper, and salt. Coat each fish piece in the egg mixture, then dredge in the flour mixture, coating all sides well.

Spray a baking dish with nonstick cooking spray. Place in the fish fillets, pour ¼ cup of water and grease with cooking spray. Place the potatoes in the pot and cover with water and place a trivet over the potatoes.

Lay the baking dish on top and seal the lid. Cook on High Pressure for 15 minutes. Do a quick release. Drain and crush the potatoes with olive oil and serve with the fish.

Seafood Spicy Penne

Servings: 4 | Prep + Cook Time: 20 minutes

INGREDIENTS

- 1 tbsp olive oil
- 1 onion, diced
- 16 ounces penne
- 24 ounces Arrabbiata sauce
- 3 cups chicken broth
- ½ tsp freshly ground black pepper
- ½ tsp salt
- 16 ounces scallops
- ¼ cup parmesan cheese, grated
- Basil leaves for garnish

DIRECTIONS

Heat oil on Sauté and stir-fry onion for 5 minutes. Stir in penne, arrabbiata sauce, and 2 cups of broth. Season with the black pepper and.

Seal the lid and cook for 6 minutes on High Pressure. Do a quick release. Remove to a plate. Pour the remaining broth and add scallops. Stir to coat, seal the lid and cook on High Pressure for 4 minutes.

Do a quick release. Mix in the pasta and serve topped with parmesan cheese and basil leaves.

Shrimp Farfalle with Spinach

Servings: 4 | Prep + Cook Time: 20 minutes

INGREDIENTS

1¼ pounds shrimp, peeled and deveined
1½ tsp salt
1 tbsp melted butter
2 garlic cloves, minced
¼ cup white wine
10 ounces farfalle

2½ cups water
⅓ cup tomato puree
½ tsp red chili flakes or to taste
1 tsp grated lemon zest
1 tbsp lemon juice
6 cups spinach

DIRECTIONS

On Sauté, pour white wine, bring to simmer for 2 minutes to reduce the liquid by half. Stir in the farfalle, water, salt, garlic, puréed tomato, shrimp, melted butter, and chili flakes. Seal the lid. Cook for 5 minutes on High pressure. Do a quick release. Stir in lemon zest, juice, and spinach until wilted and soft.

Mussel Chowder with Oyster Crackers

Servings: 4 | Prep + Cook Time: 20 minutes

INGREDIENTS

2 cups low carb oyster crackers
2 tbsp olive oil
¼ cup finely grated Pecorino Romano cheese
½ tsp garlic powder
Salt and pepper to taste
2 pancetta slices
2 celery stalks, chopped
1 medium onion, chopped
1 tbsp flour

¼ cup white wine
1 cup water
20 ounces canned mussels, drained, liquid reserved
1 pound potatoes, peeled and cut chunks
1 tsp dried rosemary
1 bay leaf
1½ cups heavy cream
2 tbsp chopped fresh chervil

DIRECTIONS

Fry pancetta on Sauté for 5 minutes, until crispy. Remove to a paper towel–lined plate and set aside. Sauté the celery and onion in the same fat for 1 minute, stirring, until the vegetables soften.

Mix in the flour to coat the vegetables. Pour in the wine simmer. Cook for about 1 minute or until reduced by about one-third. Pour in the water, the reserved mussel liquid, potatoes, salt, rosemary, and bay leaf.

Seal the lid and cook on High Pressure for 4 minutes. Do a natural pressure release for 5 minutes. Stir in the mussels and heavy cream. Press Sauté and bring the soup to a simmer to heat the mussels through.

Discard the bay leaf. Spoon the soup into bowls and crumble the pancetta over the top. Garnish with the chervil and crackers, on side.

Crabmeat with Asparagus & Broccoli Pilaf

Servings: 4 | Prep + Cook Time: 20 minutes

INGREDIENTS

½ pound asparagus, trimmed and cut into 1-inch pieces
½ pound broccoli florets
Salt to taste
2 tbsp olive oil
1 small onion, chopped (about ½ cup)
1 cup rice
⅓ cup white wine
3 cups vegetable stock
8 ounces lump crabmeat

DIRECTIONS

Heat oil on Sauté and cook onions for 3 minutes, until soft. Stir in rice and cook for 1 minute. Pour in the wine. Cook for 2 to 3 minutes, stirring, until the liquid has almost evaporated.

Add vegetable stock and salt; stir to combine. Place a trivet atop. Arrange the broccoli and asparagus on the trivet. Seal the lid and cook on High Pressure for 8 minutes. Do a quick release.

Remove the vegetables to a bowl. Fluff the rice with a fork and add in the crabmeat, heat for a minute. Taste and adjust the seasoning. Serve immediately topped with broccoli and asparagus.

Italian Salmon with Creamy Polenta

Servings: 4 | Prep + Cook Time: 20 minutes

INGREDIENTS

1 cup corn grits polenta
½ cup milk
3 cups chicken stock
3 tbsp butter
Salt to taste
3 tbsp Italian seasoning
1 tbsp sugar
4 salmon fillets, skin removed
Cooking spray

DIRECTIONS

Combine polenta, milk, chicken stock, butter, and salt in the pot. Stir and bring mixture to boil on Sauté.

In a bowl mix Italian seasoning, sugar, and salt. Oil the fillets with cooking spray and add the spice mixture. Insert a trivet and arrange the fillets on top. Seal the lid and cook on High Pressure for 9 minutes.

Do a natural pressure release for 10 minutes. Stir and serve immediately with the salmon.

Orange Salmon Fillets

Servings: 3 | Prep + Cook Time: 17 minutes

INGREDIENTS

1 lb salmon filets
1 cup orange juice, freshly squeezed
2 tbsp cornstarch
1 tsp himalayan pink salt
½ tsp black pepper, freshly ground
½ tsp garlic, minced
1 tsp orange zest, freshly grated

DIRECTIONS

Add all ingredients and seal the lid. Cook on High pressure for 10 minutes.

Do a quick pressure release.

Garlic-Lemon Salmon Steak

Servings: 3 | Prep + Cook Time: 65 minutes

INGREDIENTS

1 lb salmon steaks
1 tsp garlic powder
½ tsp rosemary powder
1 cup olive oil

½ cup apple cider vinegar
1 tsp salt
¼ cup lemon juice
½ tsp white pepper

DIRECTIONS

In a bowl, mix garlic, rosemary, olive oil, apple cider vinegar, salt, lemon juice, and pepper. Pour the mixture into a Ziploc bag along with the salmon. Seal the bag and shake to coat well. Refrigerate for 30 minutes. Pour in 3 cups of water in the instant pot and insert the trivet. Remove the fish from the Ziploc bag and place on top.

Reserve the marinade. Seal lid and cook on Steam mode for 15 minutes on High Pressure. When ready, do a quick release and remove the steaks. Discard the liquid and wipe clean the pot. Grease with some of the marinade and hit Sauté. Add salmon steaks and brown on both sides for 3-4 minutes.

Crispy Herbed Trout

Servings: 2 | Prep + Cook Time: 30 minutes

INGREDIENTS

1 lb fresh trout (2 pieces)
2 cups fish stock
1 tbsp fresh mint, chopped
¼ tsp dried thyme, ground
1 tbsp fresh parsley, chopped

3 garlic cloves, chopped
3 tbsp olive oil
2 tbsp fresh lemon juice
1 tsp sea salt

DIRECTIONS

In a bowl, mix mint, thyme, parsley, garlic, olive oil, lemon juice, chili, and salt. Stir to combine. Spread the abdominal cavity of the fish and brush with the marinade. Then, brush the fish from the outside and set aside.

Insert the trivet in instant pot. Pour in the stock and place the fish on top. Seal the lid and cook on Steam mode for 15 minutes on High Pressure. Do a quick release and serve immediately.

Garlicky Seafood Pasta

Servings: 4 | Prep + Cook Time: 30 minutes

INGREDIENTS

1 lb fresh seafood mix
¼ cup olive oil
4 garlic cloves, crushed
1 tbsp fresh parsley, chopped

1 tsp fresh rosemary, chopped
½ tbsp white wine
1 tsp salt
1 lb squid ink pasta

DIRECTIONS

Heat 3 tbsp olive oil on Sauté and stir-fry the garlic, for 1 minute, until fragrant. Add seafood, parsley, rosemary, and salt. Give it a stir. Add the remaining oil, wine, and ½ cup of water. Seal the lid and cook on High for 4 minutes. Do a quick release and set aside.

Follow the instructions to prepare the pasta. Open the instant pot, add the pasta, give it a final stir, and serve hot.

Green Mackerel with Potatoes

Servings: 4 | Prep + Cook Time: 32 minutes

INGREDIENTS

4 mackerels, skin on
1 lb of fresh spinach, torn
5 potatoes, peeled and chopped
¼ cup olive oil,
2 garlic cloves, crushed

1 tsp dried rosemary, chopped
2 sprigs of fresh mint leaves, chopped
1 lemon, juiced
Sea salt to taste

DIRECTIONS

Grease the pot with 4 tbsp olive oil. Stir-fry garlic and rosemary on Sauté, for 1 minute. Stir in spinach, a pinch of salt and cook for 4-5 minutes, until soft. Remove the spinach from the cooker and set aside.

Add the remaining oil to and make a layer of potatoes. Top with fish and drizzle with lemon juice, olive oil, and sea salt. Pour in 1 cup of water, seal the lid and cook on Steam mode for 7 minutes on High.

When ready, do a quick release. Plate the fish and potatoes with spinach, and serve immediately.

Herbs & Lemon Stuffed Tench

Servings: 2 | Prep + Cook Time: 20 minutes

INGREDIENTS

1 tench, cleaned and gutted
1 lemon, quartered
2 tbsp olive oil
1 tsp fresh rosemary, chopped

¼ tsp dried thyme, ground
2 garlic cloves, crushed
½ tsp sea salt

DIRECTIONS

In a bowl, mix olive oil, rosemary, thyme, garlic, and salt. Stir to combine. Brush the fish with the previously prepared mixture and stuff with lemon slices.

Pour 2 cups of water into the instant pot, set the steamer tray and place the fish on top. Seal the lid and cook on Steam for 15 minutes on High. Do a quick release. For a crispier taste, briefly brown the fish in a grill pan.

Quick Salmon Fillets

Servings: 4 | Prep + Cook Time: 15 minutes

INGREDIENTS

4 salmon fillets
1 cup lemon juice
2 tbsp butter, softened

2 tbsp dill
¼ tsp salt
¼ tsp pepper, freshly ground

DIRECTIONS

Sprinkle the fillets with salt and pepper. Insert the steamer tray and place the salmon on top. Pour in the lemon juice and 2 cups of water. Seal the lid.

Cook on Steam mode for 5 minutes on High. When done, release the Pressure naturally, for 10 minutes. Set aside the salmon and discard the liquid.

Wipe the pot clean and press Sauté. Add butter and briefly brown the fillets on both sides – for 3-4 minutes. Sprinkle with dill, to serve.

Fish Stew

Servings: 6 | Prep + Cook Time: 30 minutes

INGREDIENTS

2 lb of different fish and seafood
¼ tbsp olive oil
2 onions, peeled, chopped
2 carrots, grated

A handful of fresh parsley, finely chopped
2 garlic cloves, crushed
3 cups water
1 tsp sea salt

DIRECTIONS

Heat 3 tbsp olive oil on Sauté. Stir-fry onion and garlic, for 3-4 minutes, or until translucent. Add the remaining ingredients. Seal the lid, and cook on High Pressure for 10 minutes. Do a quick release.

Lemon & Dill Salmon with Greens

Servings: 4 | Prep + Cook Time: 30 minutes

INGREDIENTS

1 lb salmon filets, boneless
1 lb fresh spinach, torn
4 tbsp olive oil
2 garlic cloves, chopped

2 tbsp lemon juice
1 tbsp fresh dill, chopped
1 tsp sea salt
¼ tsp black pepper, ground

DIRECTIONS

Place spinach in the pot, cover with water and lay the trivet on top. Rub the salmon filets with half of the olive oil, dill, salt, pepper and garlic. Lay on the trivet. Seal the lid and cook on Steam for 5 minutes on High.

Do a quick release. Remove salmon to a serving plate. Drain the spinach in a colander. Serve the fish on a bed of spinach. Season with salt and drizzle with lemon juice.

Marinated Squid in White Wine Sauce

Servings: 3 | Prep + Cook Time: 45 minutes

INGREDIENTS

1 lb fresh squid rings
1 cup dry white wine
1 cup olive oil
2 garlic cloves, crushed
1 lemon, juiced

2 cups fish stock
¼ tsp red pepper flakes
¼ tsp dried oregano
1 tbsp fresh rosemary, chopped
1 tsp sea salt

DIRECTIONS

In a bowl, mix wine, olive oil, lemon juice, garlic, flakes, oregano, rosemary, and salt. Submerge squid rings in this mixture and cover with a lid.

Refrigerate for 1 hour. Remove the squid from the fridge and place them in the pot along with stock and half of the marinade. Seal the lid.

Cook on High Pressure for 6 minutes. Release the Pressure naturally, for 10 minutes. Transfer the rings to a plate and drizzle with some marinade to serve.

Octopus & Shrimp with Collard Greens

Servings: 4 | Prep + Cook Time: 35 minutes

INGREDIENTS

- 1 lb collard greens, chopped
- 1 lb shrimp, whole
- 6 oz octopus, cut into bite-sized pieces
- 1 large tomato, peeled, chopped
- 3 cups fish stock
- 4 tbsp olive oil
- 3 garlic cloves
- 2 tbsp fresh parsley, chopped
- 1 tsp sea salt

DIRECTIONS

Place shrimp and octopus in the pot. Add tomato and fish stock. Seal the lid and cook on High Pressure for 15 minutes. Do a quick release. Remove shrimp and octopus, drain the liquid.

Heat olive oil on Sauté and add garlic, parsley, and stir-fry until translucent. Add collard greens and simmer for 10 minutes. Season with salt, stir and remove from the cooker. Serve with shrimp and octopus.

Anchovy & Mussel Rice

Servings: 4 | Prep + Cook Time: 40 minutes

INGREDIENTS

- 1 cup rice
- 6 oz mussels
- 1 onion, finely chopped
- 1 garlic clove, crushed
- 1 tbsp dried rosemary, finely chopped
- ¼ cup salted capers
- 1 tsp chili pepper, ground
- ½ tsp salt
- 3 tbsp olive oil
- 4 salted anchovies

DIRECTIONS

Add rice to the pot, and pour 2 cups of water. Seal the lid and cook on Rice mode for 8 minutes on High.

Do a quick release. Remove the rice and set aside. Grease the pot with oil, and stir-fry garlic and onions, for 2 minutes, on Sauté. Add mussels and rosemary. Cook for 10 more minutes. Stir in rice and season with salt and chili pepper. Serve with anchovies and capers.

Steamed Sea Bream

Servings: 4 | Prep + Cook Time: 50 minutes

INGREDIENTS

- 2 pieces sea bream (2 lb), cleaned
- ¼ cup olive oil
- ¼ cup freshly squeezed lemon juice
- 1 tbsp fresh thyme sprigs
- 1 tbsp Italian Seasoning mix
- ½ tsp sea salt
- 1 tsp garlic powder
- 4 cups fish stock

DIRECTIONS

In a bowl, mix oil, lemon juice, thyme, Italian seasoning, sea salt, and garlic powder. Brush onto fish and wrap tightly with a plastic foil. Refrigerate for 30 minutes before cooking. Pour fish stock in the pot.

Set the steamer rack and place the fish on top. Seal the lid. Cook on Steam mode for 8 minutes on High. Do a quick release, open the lid, and unwrap the fish. Serve immediately with steam vegetables.

Rosemary & Dill Trout Fillet

Servings: 6 | Prep + Cook Time: 1 hour 20 minutes

INGREDIENTS

2 lb trout fillets, skin on
½ cup olive oil
¼ cup apple cider vinegar
1 red onion, chopped
1 lemon, sliced
2 garlic cloves, crushed

1 tbsp fresh rosemary, chopped
1 tbsp dill sprigs, chopped
½ sea salt
¼ tsp freshly ground black pepper
3 cups fish stock

DIRECTIONS

In a bowl, mix oil, apple cider, onions, garlic, rosemary, dill, sea salt, and pepper. Submerge the fillets into this mixture and Refrigerate for 1 hour. Grease the bottom of the pot with 4 tbsp of the marinade and pour in the stock. Add the fish, seal the lid and cook on High pressure for 4 minutes. Do a quick release.

Red Pollock & Tomato Stew

Servings: 4 | Prep + Cook Time: 50 minutes

INGREDIENTS

1 lb pollock fillet
4 cloves, crushed
1 lb tomatoes, peeled and chopped
2 bay leaves, whole
2 cups fish stock

1 tsp freshly ground black pepper
1 onion, peeled and finely chopped
½ cup olive oil
1 tsp sea salt

DIRECTIONS

Heat 2 tbsp olive oil on Sauté. Add onion and sauté until translucent, stirring constantly, for about 3-4 minutes. Add tomatoes and cook until soft. Press Cancel. Add the remaining ingredients and seal the lid. Cook on High pressure for 15 minutes. When ready, do a quick release and serve warm.

Squid Ink Pasta with Trout Fillets

Servings: 5 | Prep + Cook Time: 25 minutes

INGREDIENTS

1 lb squid ink pasta
6 oz trout fillet
1 cup olive oil
½ cup lemon juice
1 tsp fresh rosemary, chopped

3 garlic cloves, crushed, halved
2 tsp sea salt
2 tbsp fresh parsley, finely chopped
A handful of olives and capers for serving

DIRECTIONS

In a bowl, mix oil, lemon juice, rosemary, 2 garlic cloves, and 1 teaspoon of salt. Stir well and submerge fillets in this mixture. Refrigerate for 30 minutes. Remove from the fridge and drain, reserving the liquid.

Grease the pot with some of the marinade. Add fillets, 1 cup of water, and 3 tablespoons of the marinade. Seal the lid and cook on High pressure for 4 minutes. Do a quick release, add the pasta and 1 cup of water.

Seal the lid and cook for 3 minutes on High pressure. Do a quick release. Serve with capers and olives.

Marinated Smelt with Mustard Rice

Servings: 4 | Prep + Cook Time: 35 minutes

INGREDIENTS

1 lb fresh smelt, cleaned, heads removed
1 cup extra virgin olive oil
½ cup freshly squeezed lemon juice
¼ cup freshly squeezed orange juice
1 tbsp Dijon mustard
1 tsp fresh rosemary, finely chopped
2 garlic cloves, crushed
1 tsp sea salt

½ tbsp rice
5 oz okra
1 carrot, chopped
¼ cup green peas, soaked overnight
5 oz cherry tomatoes, halved
4 tbsp vegetable oil
2 cups fish stock

DIRECTIONS

In a bowl, mix oil, juices, dijon, garlic, salt, and rosemary. Stir well and submerge fish in this mixture.

Refrigerate for 1 hour. Meanwhile, heat oil on Sauté and stir-fry carrot, peas, cherry tomatoes, and okra, for 10 minutes. Add rice and fish stock. Seal the lid and cook on Rice for 8 minutes on High.

Do a quick release and add in the fish along with half of the marinade. Seal the lid again and cook on Steam for 4 minutes on High. Release the pressure naturally, for 10 minutes. Serve immediately.

Thick Fish Soup

Servings: 4 | Prep + Cook Time: 45 minutes

INGREDIENTS

6 oz mackerel fillets
½ cup wheat groats, soaked
½ cup kidney beans, soaked
¼ cup sweet corn
1 lb tomatoes, peeled, roughly chopped

4 cups fish stock
4 tbsp olive oil
1 tsp sea salt
1 tsp fresh rosemary, finely chopped
2 garlic cloves, crushed

DIRECTIONS

Heat olive oil on Sauté, and stir-fry tomatoes and garlic for 5 minutes. Add rosemary, stock, salt, corn, kidney beans, and wheat groats. Seal the lid and cook on High Pressure for 25 minutes.

Do a quick release and add mackerel fillets. Seal the lid and cook on Steam for 8 minutes on High. Do a quick release, open the lid and serve immediately drizzled with freshly squeezed lemon juice.

White Wine Catfish Fillets

Servings: 3 | Prep + Cook Time: 50 minutes

INGREDIENTS

1 lb catfish fillet
1 lemon, juiced
½ cup parsley leaves, chopped
2 garlic cloves, crushed
1 onion, finely chopped
1 tbsp fresh dill, chopped

1 tbsp fresh rosemary
2 cups white wine
2 tbsp Dijon mustard
1 cup extra virgin olive oil
3 cups fish stock

DIRECTIONS

In a bowl, mix lemon juice, parsley, garlic, onion, fresh dill, rosemary, wine, mustard, and oil. Stir well to combine. Submerge fillets in this mixture and cover with a tight lid. Refrigerate for 1 hour.

Insert the trivet, remove the fish from the fridge and place it on the rack. Pour in stock along with the marinade and seal the lid. Cook on Steam for 8 minutes on High. Release the pressure quickly and serve.

Trout & Spinach with Tomato Sauce

Servings: 3 | Prep + Cook Time: 55 minutes

INGREDIENTS

1 lb trout fillets
6 oz fresh spinach, torn
2 tomatoes, peeled, diced
3 cups fish stock
1 tsp dried thyme

½ tsp fresh rosemary
¼ cup olive oil
¼ cup freshly squeezed Lime juice
1 tsp sea salt
2 garlic cloves, crushed

DIRECTIONS

Rinse the fillets and sprinkle them with sea salt. In a bowl, mix olive oil, thyme, rosemary, and lime juice. Stir well and submerge fillets in this mixture. Refrigerate for 30 minutes; then drain the fillets.

Reserve the marinade, grease the pot with 3 tbsp of the marinade and add the fillets and stock.

Seal the lid and cook on Steam for 8 minutes on High Pressure. Do a quick release, remove the fish and set aside. Add the remaining marinade to the pot. Hit Sauté and add the tomatoes and spinach. Cook until soft. Give it a good stir and remove to a plate. Add fish, drizzle with tomato sauce and serve warm.

Tuna & Rosemary Pizza

Servings: 4 | Prep + Cook Time: 25 minutes

INGREDIENTS

1 cup canned tuna, oil-free
½ cup mozzarella cheese, shredded
¼ cup goat's cheese
3 tbsp olive oil

1 tbsp tomato paste
½ tsp dried rosemary
14 oz pizza crust
1 cup olives, optional

DIRECTIONS

Grease the bottom of a baking dish with one tablespoon of olive oil. Line some parchment paper. Flour the working surface and roll out the pizza dough to the approximate size of your instant pot. Gently fit the dough in the previously prepared baking dish.

In a bowl, combine olive oil, tomato paste and rosemary. Whisk together and spread the mixture over the crust.

Sprinkle with goat cheese, mozzarella, and tuna. Place a trivet inside the pot and pour in 1 cup of water.

Seal the lid, and cook for 15 minutes on High Pressure. Do a quick release. Remove the pizza from the pot. Cut and serve.

Chili & Oregano Salmon Fillet

Servings: 4 | Prep + Cook Time: 60 minutes

INGREDIENTS

1 lb fresh salmon fillets, skin on
¼ cup olive oil
½ cup freshly squeezed lemon juice
2 garlic cloves, crushed

1 tbsp fresh oregano leaves, chopped
1 tsp sea salt
¼ tsp chili flakes
2 cups fish stock

DIRECTIONS

In a bowl, mix oil, lemon juice, garlic, oregano leaves, salt, and flakes. Brush the fillets with the mixture and refrigerate for 30 minutes. Pour the stock in, and insert the trivet. Pat-dry the salmon and place on the steamer rack. Seal the lid, and cook on Steam for 10 minutes on High. Do a quick release and serve.

Garlic Seafood with Brown Rice

Servings: 4 | Prep + Cook Time: 30 minutes

INGREDIENTS

1 lb frozen seafood mix
1 cup brown rice
1 tbsp calamari ink
2 tbsp extra virgin olive oil
2 garlic cloves, crushed

1 tbsp finely chopped rosemary
½ tsp salt
3 cups fish stock
Freshly squeezed lemon juice

DIRECTIONS

Add in all ingredients, Seal the lid and cook on Rice mode for 10 minutes on High. Release the pressure naturally, for 10 minutes. Squeeze lemon juice and serve.

Citrusy Marinated Grilled Catfish

Servings: 4 | Prep + Cook Time: 60 minutes

INGREDIENTS

1 lb flathead catfish
1 cup orange juice
¼ cup lemon juice
½ cup olive oil
1 tbsp dried thyme

1 tbsp dried rosemary
1 tsp chili flakes
1 tsp sea salt
3 cups fish stock

DIRECTIONS

In a bowl, mix orange juice, lemon juice, olive oil, thyme, rosemary, chili flakes, and salt. Brush the fish with this mixture and Refrigerate for 30 minutes. Remove from the fridge, drain; reserve the marinade.

Insert the trivet in the pot. Pour in stock and marinade, and place the fish onto the top. Seal the lid and cook on High Pressure for 10 minutes. Do a quick release and serve immediately.

VEGETABLES & VEGAN

Green Minestrone

Servings: 4 | Prep + Cook Time: 30 minutes

INGREDIENTS

2 tbsp olive oil
1 head broccoli, cut into florets
4 celery stalks, chopped thinly
1 leek, chopped thinly
1 zucchini, chopped
1 cup green beans

2 cups vegetable broth
3 whole black peppercorns
Salt to taste
water to cover
2 cups chopped kale

DIRECTIONS

Add broccoli, leek, beans, salt, peppercorns, zucchini, and celery. Mix in vegetable broth, oil, and water. Seal the lid and cook on High Pressure for 4 minutes. Release pressure naturally for 5 minutes, then release the remaining pressure quickly. Stir in kale; set on Sauté, and cook until tender.

Vegan Carrot Gazpacho

Servings: 4 | Prep + Cook Time: 2 hours 30 minutes

INGREDIENTS

1 pound trimmed carrots
1 pound tomatoes, chopped
1 cucumber, peeled and chopped
¼ cup olive oil
2 tbsp lemon juice

1 red onion, chopped
2 cloves garlic
2 tbsp white wine vinegar
Salt and freshly ground black pepper to taste

DIRECTIONS

Add carrots, salt and enough water. Seal the lid and cook for 20 minutes on High Pressure. Do a quick release. Set the beets to a bowl and place in the refrigerator to cool. In a blender, add carrots, cucumber, red onion, pepper, garlic, oil, tomatoes, lemon juice, vinegar, and salt. Blend until very smooth. Place gazpacho to a serving bowl, chill while covered for 2 hours.

Green Beans with Feta & Nuts

Servings: 6 | Prep + Cook Time: 15 minutes

INGREDIENTS

Juice from 1 lemon
1½ cups water
2 pounds green beans, trimmed
1 cup chopped toasted pine nuts

1 cup feta cheese, crumbled
6 tbsp olive oil
½ tsp salt
Black pepper to taste

DIRECTIONS

Add water and set the rack over the water and the steamer basket on the rack. Loosely heap green beans into the steamer basket. Seal lid and cook on High Pressure for 5 minutes. Release pressure quickly. Drop green beans into a salad bowl. Top with the olive oil, feta cheese, pepper, and pine nuts.

Garlic Veggie Mash with Parmesan

Servings: 6 | Prep + Cook Time: 15 minutes

INGREDIENTS

3 pounds Yukon Gold potatoes, chopped
1 ½ cups cauliflower, broken into florets
1 carrot, chopped
1 cup Parmesan Cheese, shredded
¼ cup butter, melted

¼ cup milk
1 tsp salt
1 garlic clove, minced
Fresh parsley for garnish

DIRECTIONS

Into the pot, add veggies, salt and cover with enough water. Seal the lid and cook on High Pressure for 10 minutes. Release the pressure quickly. Drain the vegetables and mash them with a potato masher.

Add garlic, butter and milk, and Whisk until everything is well incorporated. Serve topped with Parmesan cheese and chopped parsley.

Pesto Arborio Rice Bowls with Veggies

Servings: 2 | Prep + Cook Time: 30 minutes

INGREDIENTS

1 cup arborio rice, rinsed
2 cups water
salt and ground black pepper to taste
1 small beet, peeled and cubed
1 cup broccoli florets

1 carrot, peeled and chopped
½ pound Brussels sprouts
2 eggs
¼ cup pesto sauce
lemon wedges, for serving

DIRECTIONS

In the pot, mix water, salt, rice and pepper. Set trivet over rice and set steamer basket on top. To the steamer basket, add eggs, Brussels sprouts, broccoli, beet cubes, carrots, pepper and salt.

Seal the lid and cook for 1 minute on High Pressure. Release pressure naturally for 10 minutes, then release any remaining pressure quickly. Remove steamer basket and trivet from the pot and set the eggs to a bowl of ice water. Peel and halve the eggs. Use a fork to fluff the rice.

Separate rice, broccoli, carrots, beet, Brussels sprouts, eggs, and a dollop of pesto into two bowls. Serve alongside a lemon wedge.

Italian Vegetable Stew

Servings: 4 | Prep + Cook Time: 25 minutes

INGREDIENTS

3 zucchini, peeled, chopped
1 eggplant, peeled, chopped
3 red bell peppers, chopped
½ cup fresh tomato juice

2 tsp Italian Seasoning
½ tsp salt
2 tbsp olive oil

DIRECTIONS

Add all ingredients and give it a good stir. Pour 1 cup of water. Seal the lid and cook on High pressure for 15 minutes. Do a quick release. Set aside to cool completely. Serve as a cold salad or a side dish.

Mashed Potatoes with Spinach

Servings: 6 | Prep + Cook Time: 30 minutes

INGREDIENTS

3 pounds potatoes, peeled and quartered
1½ cups water
½ cup milk
⅓ cup butter
2 tbsp chopped fresh chives
Salt and black pepper to taste
2 cups spinach, chopped

DIRECTIONS

In the cooker, mix water, salt and potatoes. Seal the lid and cook on High Pressure for 8 minutes. Release the pressure quickly. Drain the potatoes, and reserve the liquid in a bowl. In a bowl, mash the potatoes.

Mix with butter and milk; season with pepper and salt. With reserved cooking liquid, thin the potatoes to attain the desired consistency. Put the spinach in the remaining potato liquid and stir until wilted; Season to taste. Drain and serve with potato mash. Garnish with cracked black pepper and chives.

Herby-Garlic Potatoes

Servings: 4 | Prep + Cook Time: 30 minutes

INGREDIENTS

1½ pounds potatoes
3 tbsp butter
3 cloves garlic, thinly chopped
2 tbsp fresh rosemary, chopped
½ tsp fresh thyme, chopped
½ tsp fresh parsley, chopped
¼ tsp ground black pepper
½ cup vegetable broth

DIRECTIONS

Use a small knife to pierce each potato to ensure there are no blowouts when placed under pressure. Melt butter on Sauté. Add in potatoes, rosemary, parsley, pepper, thyme, and garlic, and cook for 10 minutes until potatoes are browned and the mixture is aromatic.

In a bowl, mix miso paste and vegetable stock. Stir in to the mixture in the instant pot. Seal the lid and cook for 5 minutes on High Pressure. Release the pressure quickly.

Mushroom & Rice Stuffed Bell peppers

Servings: 4 | Prep + Cook Time: 35 minutes

INGREDIENTS

5 bell peppers, seeds and stems removed
1 onion, peeled, chopped
6 oz button mushrooms, chopped
4 garlic cloves, peeled, crushed
4 tbsp olive oil
1 tsp salt
¼ tsp freshly ground black pepper
1 cup rice
½ tbsp of paprika
2 cups vegetable stock

DIRECTIONS

Warm 2 tbsp of olive oil on Sauté. Add onions and garlic, and stir-fry until fragrant and translucent, for about 2 minutes. Press Cancel and set aside. In a bowl, combine rice and mushrooms with the mixture from the pot. Season with salt, pepper, and paprika, and stuff each bell pepper with this mixture.

Place them in the instant pot, filled side up, and pour in broth. Seal the lid and cook on High for 15 minutes. Release the pressure naturally for about 5 minutes.

Steamed Artichokes with Lemon Aioli

Servings: 4 | Prep + Cook Time: 20 minutes

INGREDIENTS

4 artichokes, trimmed
1 lemon, halved
1 tsp lemon zest
1 tbsp lemon juice
3 cloves garlic, crushed

½ cup mayonnaise
1 cup water
Salt to taste
1 handful parsley, chopped

DIRECTIONS

On artichokes' cut ends, rub with lemon. Add water into the pot. Set steamer rack over water and set steamer basket on top. Place artichokes into the basket with the points upwards; sprinkled with salt.

Seal lid and cook on high Pressure for 10 minutes. Release the pressure quickly. In a mixing bowl, combine mayonnaise, garlic, lemon juice, and lemon zest. Season to taste with salt.

Serve with warm steamed artichokes sprinkled with parsley.

Artichoke with Garlic Mayo

Servings: 4 | Prep + Cook Time: 20 minutes

INGREDIENTS

2 large artichokes
2 cups water
2 garlic cloves, smashed

½ cup mayonnaise
Salt and black pepper to taste
Juice of 1 Lime

DIRECTIONS

Using a serrated knife, trim about 1 inch from the artichokes' top. Into the pot, add water and set trivet over. Lay the artichokes on the trivet. Seal lid and cook for 14 minutes on High Pressure.

Release the pressure quickly. Mix the mayonnaise with garlic and lime juice. Season with salt and pepper. Serve artichokes in a platter with garlic mayo on the side.

Green Lasagna Soup

Servings: 4 | Prep + Cook Time: 30 minutes

INGREDIENTS

1 tsp olive oil
1 cup leeks, chopped
2 garlic cloves minced
1 cup tomato paste
1 cup tomatoes, chopped
1 carrot, chopped

½ pound broccoli, chopped
¼ cup dried green lentils
2 tsp Italian seasoning
Salt to taste
2 cups vegetable broth
3 lasagna noodles

DIRECTIONS

Warm oil on Sauté mode. Add garlic and leeks and cook for 2 minutes until soft; add tomato paste, carrot, Italian seasoning, broccoli, tomatoes, lentils, and salt. Stir in vegetable broth and lasagna pieces.

Seal the lid and cook on High Pressure for 3 minutes. Release pressure naturally for 10 minutes, then release the remaining pressure quickly. Divide soup into serving bowls and serve.

Rosemary Sweet Potato Medallions

Servings: 4 | Prep + Cook Time: 25 minutes

INGREDIENTS

1 cup water
1 tbsp fresh rosemary
1 tsp garlic powder

4 sweet potatoes
2 tbsp butter
Salt to taste

DIRECTIONS

Add water and place steamer rack over the water. Use a fork to prick sweet potatoes all over and set onto steamer rack. Seal the lid and cook on High Pressure for 12 minutes. Release the pressure quickly.

Transfer sweet potatoes to a cutting board and slice into ½-inch medallions and ensure they are peeled.

Melt butter in the on Sauté mode. Add in the medallions and cook each side for 2 to 3 minutes until browned. Season with salt and garlic powder. Serve topped with fresh rosemary.

Asparagus with Feta

Servings: 4 | Prep + Cook Time: 15 minutes

INGREDIENTS

1 cup water
1 pound asparagus spears, ends trimmed
1 tbsp olive oil

Salt and freshly ground black pepper to taste
1 lemon, cut into wedges
1 cup feta cheese, cubed

DIRECTIONS

Into the pot, add water and set trivet over the water. Place steamer basket on the trivet. Place the asparagus into the steamer basket. Seal the lid and cook on High Pressure for 1 minute.

Release the Pressure quickly. Add olive oil in a bowl and toss in asparagus until well coated. Season with pepper and salt. Serve alongside feta cheese and lemon wedges.

Quick Greek Dolmades

Servings: 4 | Prep + Cook Time: 60 minutes

INGREDIENTS

32 wine leaves, fresh or in a jar
1 cup long grain rice, rinsed
½ cup olive oil
2 garlic cloves, crushed

¼ cup freshly squeezed lemon juice
2 tbsp fresh mint
Salt and pepper to taste

DIRECTIONS

In a bowl, mix rice with 3 tbsp of olive oil, garlic, mint, salt, and pepper. Place 1 wine leaf at a time on a working surface and add 1 tsp of filling at the bottom.

Fold the leaf over the filling towards the center. Bring the 2 sides in towards the center and roll them up tightly. Grease the instant pot with 2 tbsp olive oil.

Make a layer of wine leaves and then Transfer the previously prepared rolls. Add the remaining olive oil, 2 cups of water, and lemon juice. Seal the lid and cook on High Pressure for to 30 minutes. Do a natural release, for about 10 minutes. Remove the dolmades from the pot and chill overnight.

Potato Balls in Marinara Sauce

Servings: 4 | Prep + Cook Time: 30 minutes

INGREDIENTS

2 potatoes, peeled
1 onion, peeled, chopped
1 lb fresh spinach, torn
¼ cup mozzarella cheese, shredded
2 eggs, beaten
½ tsp salt

¼ tsp freshly ground black pepper
1 tsp dried oregano, crushed
1 cup whole milk
¼ cup flour
¼ cup corn flour

Marinara Sauce:
1 lb fresh tomatoes, peeled, roughly chopped
1 large onion, peeled, chopped
2 garlic cloves, peeled, crushed
3 tbsp olive oil
¼ cup white wine

1 tsp sugar
1 tbsp dried rosemary, crushed
½ tsp salt
1 tbsp tomato paste

DIRECTIONS

Place the potatoes in your instant pot and add enough water to cover. Seal the lid and cook on High Pressure for 13 minutes. Do a quick release. Add 1 cup of milk and mash with a potato masher.

Whisk in eggs, one at the time and mix well. Add the remaining ingredients and mix with hands. Shape into balls and set aside. Press Sauté, warm olive oil and stir-fry onions, garlic, until translucent.

Stir in tomatoes and cook until tender, for about 10 minutes. Pour in wine, add sugar, rosemary, and salt. Stir in 1 tbsp of tomato paste and mix well. Cook for five more minutes. Place the potato balls in the cooker and seal with the lid. Cook on High Pressure for 5 minutes. Do a natural release, for 5 minutes.

Arugula Pizza

Servings: 4 | Prep + Cook Time: 20 minutes

INGREDIENTS

1 pizza crust
½ cup tomato paste
¼ cup water
1 tsp sugar
1 tsp dried oregano

4 oz button mushrooms, chopped
½ cup grated gouda cheese
2 tbsp extra virgin olive oil
12 Olives
1 cup arugula for serving

DIRECTIONS

Grease the bottom of a baking dish with one tablespoon of olive oil. Line some parchment paper. Flour the working surface and roll out the pizza dough to the approximate size of your instant pot. Gently fit the dough in the previously prepared baking dish.

In a bowl, combine tomato paste, water, sugar, and dry oregano. Spread the mixture over dough, make a layer with button mushrooms and grated gouda.

Add a trivet inside the pot and pour in 1 cup of water. Seal the lid, and cook for 15 minutes on High Pressure. Do a quick release. Remove the pizza from your pot using a parchment paper. Sprinkle with the remaining olive oil and top with olives and arugula. Cut and serve.

Eggplant Lasagna

Servings: 4 | Prep + Cook Time: 35 minutes

INGREDIENTS

- 1 large eggplant, chopped
- 4 oz mozzarella, chopped
- 3 oz Mascarpone cheese, at room temperature
- 2 tomatoes, chopped
- ¼ cup olive oil
- 1 tsp salt
- ½ tsp freshly ground black pepper
- 1 tsp oregano, dried

DIRECTIONS

Grease a baking dish with olive oil. Slice the eggplant and make a layer in the dish. Cover with mozzarella and tomato slices. Top with mascarpone cheese.

Repeat the process until you run out of ingredients. Meanwhile, in a bowl, mix olive oil, salt, pepper, and dried oregano.

Pour the mixture over the lasagna, and add ½ cup of water. In your inner pot, Pour 1 ½ cups of water and insert a trivet.

Lower the baking dish on the trivet, Seal the lid and cook on High Pressure for 4 minutes. When ready, do a natural release, for 10 minutes.

Spinach and Leeks with Goat Cheese

Servings: 2 | Prep + Cook Time: 10 minutes

INGREDIENTS

- 9 oz fresh spinach
- 2 leeks, chopped
- 2 red onions, chopped
- 2 garlic cloves, crushed
- ½ cup goat's cheese
- 3 tbsp olive oil
- 1 tsp kosher salt

DIRECTIONS

Grease the inner pot with oil. Stir-fry leek, garlic, and onions, for about 5 minutes, on Sauté mode. Add spinach and give it a good stir.

Season with salt and cook for 3 more minutes, stirring constantly. Press Cancel, Transfer to a serving dish and sprinkle with goat's cheese. Serve right away.

Colorful Vegetable Medley

Servings: 4 | Prep + Cook Time: 15 minutes

INGREDIENTS

- 1 cup water
- 1 small head broccoli, broken into florets
- 16 asparagus, trimmed
- 1 small head cauliflower, broken into florets
- 5 ounces green beans
- 2 carrots, peeled and cut on bias
- Salt to taste

DIRECTIONS

Add water and set trivet on top of water and place steamer basket on top. In an even layer, spread green beans, broccoli, cauliflower, asparagus, and carrots in a steamer basket. Seal the lid and cook on Steam for 3 minutes on High. Release the pressure quickly. Remove basket from the pot and season with salt.

Sweet Chickpea & Mushroom Stew

Servings: 4 | Prep + Cook Time: 20 minutes

INGREDIENTS

1 cup chickpeas, cooked
1 onion, peeled, chopped
A handful of string beans, trimmed
1 apple, cut into 1-inch cubes
½ cup raisins
½ tbsp button mushrooms, chopped
2 carrots, chopped

2 garlic cloves, crushed
4 cherry tomatoes
A handful of fresh mint
1 tsp grated ginger
½ cup freshly squeezed orange juice
½ tsp salt

DIRECTIONS

Place all ingredients in the instant pot. Pour enough water to cover. Cook on High Pressure for 8 minutes. Do a natural release, for 10 minutes.

Vegetarian Paella

Servings: 4 | Prep + Cook Time: 30 minutes

INGREDIENTS

½ cup frozen green peas
2 carrots, finely chopped
1 cup fire-roasted tomatoes
1 cup zucchini, finely chopped
½ tbsp celery root, finely chopped
6 saffron threads

1 tbsp turmeric, ground
1 tsp salt
½ tsp freshly ground black pepper
2 cup vegetable broth
1 cup long grain rice

DIRECTIONS

Place all ingredients, except rice, in the instant pot. Stir well and seal the lid. Cook on Rice mode for 8 minutes, on High. Do a quick release, open the lid and stir in the rice. Seal the lid and cook on High pressure for 3 minutes. When ready, release the pressure naturally, for about 10 minutes.

Vegetable Stew

Servings: 4 | Prep + Cook Time: 55 minutes

INGREDIENTS

1 lb potatoes, peeled, cut into bite-sized pieces
2 carrots, peeled, chopped
3 celery stalks, chopped
2 onions, peeled, chopped
1 zucchini, cut into ½ -inch thick slices
A handful of fresh celery leaves

2 tbsp butter, unsalted
3 tbsp olive oil
2 cups vegetable broth
1 tbsp paprika
1 tbsp salt
1 tsp black pepper

DIRECTIONS

Warm oil on Sauté and stir-fry the onions for 3-4 minutes, until translucent. Add carrots, celery, zucchini, and ¼ cup of broth. Continue to cook for 10 more minutes, stirring constantly.

Stir in potatoes, cayenne pepper, salt, pepper, bay leaves, remaining broth, and celery leaves. Seal the lid and cook on Meat/Stew mode for 30 minutes on High. Do a quick release and stir in 2 tbsp of butter.

Stewed Kidney Bean

Servings: 4 | Prep + Cook Time: 30 minutes

INGREDIENTS

6 oz red beans, cooked
2 carrots, chopped
2 celery stalks, cut into pieces
1 onion, peeled, chopped
2 tbsp tomato paste

1 bay leaf
2 cups vegetable broth
3 tbsp olive oil
1 tsp salt
A handful of fresh parsley

DIRECTIONS

Warm oil on Sauté and stir-fry the onions, for 3 minutes, until soft. Add celery and carrots. Cook for 5 more minutes, adding 1 tbsp of broth at the time. Add red beans, bay leaf, salt, parsley, and tomato paste.

Stir in 1 tbsp of flour and pour in the remaining broth. Seal the lid and cook on High pressure for 5 minutes on. Do a natural release, for about 10 minutes. Sprinkle with some fresh parsley and serve warm.

Lentil Spread with Parmesan

Servings: 6 | Prep + Cook Time: 15 minutes

INGREDIENTS

1 lb of lentils, cooked
1 cup sweet corn
2 tomatoes, diced
3 tbsp tomato paste
½ tsp dried oregano, ground
2 tbsp Parmesan Cheese

1 tsp salt
½ tsp red pepper flakes
3 tbsp olive oil
1 cup water
¼ cup red wine

DIRECTIONS

Heat oil on Sauté and add tomatoes, tomato paste, and ½ cup of water. Sprinkle with salt and oregano and stir-fry for 5 minutes. Press Cancel and add lentils, sweet corn, and wine.

Pour in the remaining water and seal the lid. Cook on High Pressure for 2 minutes. Do a quick release. Set aside to cool completely and refrigerate for 30 minutes. Sprinkle with Parmesan Cheese before serving.

Broccoli & Orecchiette Pasta with Feta

Servings: 4 | Prep + Cook Time: 25 minutes

INGREDIENTS

1 (9 oz) pack orecchiette
16 oz broccoli, roughly chopped
2 garlic cloves
3 tbsp olive oil

1 tbsp grated feta
1 tsp salt
¼ tsp black pepper

DIRECTIONS

Place the orecchiette and broccoli in your instant pot. Cover with water and seal the lid. Cook on High Pressure for 10 minutes. Do a quick release.

Drain the broccoli and orecchiette. Set aside. Heat the olive oil on Sauté mode. Stir-fry garlic for 2 minutes. Stir in broccoli, orecchiette, salt, and pepper. Cook for 2 more minutes. Press Cancel and stir in grated feta, to serve.

Mushroom & Spinach Cannelloni

Servings: 4 | Prep + Cook Time: 40 minutes

INGREDIENTS

1 (9 oz) pack of cannelloni
12 oz spinach, torn
6 oz button mushrooms, chopped
3 oz ricotta cheese

¼ cup milk
3 oz butter
¼ tsp salt
1 tbsp sour cream

DIRECTIONS

Melt butter on Sauté and add mushrooms. Stir well and cook until soft. Add spinach and milk, and continue to cook for 6 minutes, stirring constantly. Stir in the cheese, season to taste and press Cancel.

Line parchment paper over a baking sheet. Fill cannelloni with spinach mixture. Gently place them on the baking sheet. Pour 2 cups of water in the instant pot and insert a trivet.

Lower the baking sheet on the trivet. Seal the lid, and cook on High Pressure for 20 minutes. Do a quick release. Remove and chill for a while. Top with sour cream and serve.

Mushroom Spinach Tagliatelle

Servings: 4 | Prep + Cook Time: 25 minutes

INGREDIENTS

1 lb spinach tagliatelle
6 oz frozen mixed mushrooms
3 tbsp butter, unsalted
¼ cup feta cheese

¼ cup grated Parmesan Cheese
2 garlic cloves, crushed
¼ cup heavy cream
1 tbsp Italian Seasoning mix

DIRECTIONS

Melt butter on Sauté, and stir-fry the garlic for a minute. Stir in feta, and mushrooms. Add tagliatelle and 2 cups of water. Cook on High Pressure for 4 minutes. Quick release the pressure and top with parmesan.

Feta Cheese Stuffed Potatoes

Servings: 3 | Prep + Cook Time: 60 minutes

INGREDIENTS

6 potatoes, whole, rinsed, drained

¼ cup olive oil
3 garlic cloves, crushed
¼ cup feta cheese
1 tsp fresh rosemary, chopped

½ tsp dried thyme
2 oz button mushrooms, chopped
1 tsp salt

DIRECTIONS

Rub the potatoes with salt and place them in the instant pot. Add enough water to cover and seal the lid. Cook on High Pressure for 30 minutes. Do a quick release and remove the potatoes. Let chill for a while.

Meanwhile, in the pot, mix olive oil, garlic, rosemary, thyme, and mushrooms. Sauté until the mushrooms soften, about 5 minutes, on Sauté. Remove from the cooker and stir in feta. Cut the top of each potato and spoon out the middle. Fill with cheese mixture and serve immediately.

Leek & Garlic Cannellini Beans

Servings: 4 | Prep + Cook Time: 45 minutes

INGREDIENTS

1 lb cannellini beans, soaked overnight
1 onion, peeled, chopped
2 large leeks, finely chopped

Topping:
4 tbsp vegetable oil
2 tbsp flour

3 garlic cloves, whole
1 tsp pepper
1 tsp salt

1 tbsp cayenne pepper

DIRECTIONS

Add all ingredients, except for the topping ones, in the instant pot. Press Manual/Pressure Cook and cook for 20 minutes on High. Meanwhile, heat 4 tbsp of oil in a skillet. Add flour and cayenne pepper.

Stir-fry for 2 minutes and set aside. When you hear the cooker's end signal, do a quick release. Pour in the cayenne mixture and give it a good stir. Let it sit for 15 minutes before serving.

Mushroom & Vegetable Penne Pasta

Servings: 4 | Prep + Cook Time: 25 minutes

INGREDIENTS

6 oz penne pasta
6 oz shiitake mushrooms, chopped
2 garlic cloves, crushed
1 small carrot, cut into strips
6 oz zucchini cut into strips
6 oz finely chopped leek

4 oz fresh baby spinach, finely chopped
3 tbsp oil
2 tbsp soy sauce
1 tsp ground ginger
½ tsp salt

DIRECTIONS

Heat oil on Sauté and stir-fry carrot and garlic for 3-4 minutes. Add the remaining ingredients and pour in 2 cup of water. Cook on High Pressure for 4 minutes. Quick release the pressure and serve.

Braised Swiss Chard with Potatoes

Servings: 4 | Prep + Cook Time: 15 minutes

INGREDIENTS

1 lb Swiss chard, torn, chopped, with stems
2 potatoes, peeled, chopped

¼ tbsp oregano
1 tsp salt

DIRECTIONS

Add Swiss chard and potatoes to the pot. Pour water to cover all and sprinkle with salt. Seal the lid and select Manual/Pressure Cook.

Cook for 3 minutes on High. Release the steam naturally, for 5 minutes. Transfer to a serving plate. Sprinkle with oregano or Italian seasoning, to serve.

DESSERTS

Cinnamon Apple Crisp

Servings: 5 | Prep + Cook Time: 30 minutes

INGREDIENTS

Topping:

½ cup oat flour
½ cup old-fashioned rolled oats
½ cup granulated sugar
¼ cup olive oil

Filling:

5 apples, peeled, cored, and halved
2 tbsp arrowroot powder
½ cup water
1 tsp ground cinnamon
¼ tsp ground nutmeg
½ tsp vanilla paste

DIRECTIONS

In a bowl, combine sugar, oat flour, rolled oats, and olive oil to form coarse crumbs. Ladle the apples into the instant pot. Mix water with arrowroot powder in a bowl. Stir in salt, nutmeg, cinnamon, and vanilla.

Toss in the apples to coat. Apply oat topping to the apples. Seal the lid and cook on High Pressure for 10 minutes. Release the pressure naturally for 5 minutes, then release the remaining Pressure quickly.

Dark Chocolate Brownies

Servings: 6 | Prep + Cook Time: 40 minutes

INGREDIENTS

1 ½ cups water
2 eggs
⅓ cup granulated sugar
¼ cup olive oil
⅓ cup flour
⅓ cup cocoa powder
⅓ cup dark chocolate chips
⅓ cup chopped Walnuts
1 tbsp milk
½ tsp baking powder
1 tbsp vanilla extract
A pinch salt

DIRECTIONS

Add water and set steamer rack into the cooker. Line a parchment paper on the steamer basket. In a bowl, beat eggs and sugar to mix until smooth. Stir in oil, cocoa, milk, salt baking powder, chocolate chips, flour, walnuts, vanilla, and sea salt. Transfer the batter to the prepared steamer basket.

Arrange into an even layer. Seal the lid, press Cake and cook for 20 minutes on High Pressure. Release the pressure quickly. Let brownie cool before cutting. Use powdered sugar to dust and serve.

Cinnamon Pumpkin Pudding

Servings: 4 | Prep + Cook Time: 20 minutes

INGREDIENTS

1 lb pumpkin, peeled and chopped into bite-sized pieces
1 cup granulated sugar
½ cup cornstarch
4 cups apple juice, unsweetened
1 tsp cinnamon, ground
3-4 cloves

DIRECTIONS

In a bowl, combine sugar and apple juice until sugar dissolves completely.

Pour the mixture into the pot and stir in cornstarch, cinnamon, cloves, and pumpkin. Seal the lid, and cook for 10 minutes on High Pressure. Do a quick release. Pour in the pudding into 4 serving bowls. Let cool to room temperature and refrigerate overnight.

Flan with Whipping Cream

Servings: 4 | Prep + Cook Time: 30 minutes

INGREDIENTS

½ cup granulated sugar
4 tbsp. caramel syrup
1 cup water
3 eggs

½ tsp vanilla extract
½ tbsp milk
5 oz whipping cream

DIRECTIONS

Combine milk, whipping cream and vanilla extract in your instant pot. Press Sauté, and cook for 5 minutes, or until small bubbles form. Set aside.

Using an electric mixer, whisk the eggs and sugar. Gradually add the cream mixture and whisk until well combined. Divide the caramel syrup between 4 ramekins. Fill with egg mixture and place them on top of the trivet. Pour in water.

Seal the lid, and cook for 15 minutes on High Pressure. Do a quick release. remove the ramekins from the pot and cool completely before serving.

Nutmeg Squash Tart

Servings: 8 | Prep + Cook Time: 30 minutes

INGREDIENTS

15 oz mashed squash
6 fl oz milk
½ tsp cinnamon, ground
½ tsp nutmeg

½ tsp salt
3 large eggs
½ cup granulated sugar
1 pack pate brisee

DIRECTIONS

Place squash puree in a large bowl. Add milk, cinnamon, eggs, nutmeg, salt, and sugar. Whisk together until well incorporated. Grease a baking dish with oil.

Gently place pate brisee creating the edges with hands. Pour the squash mixture over and flatten the surface with a spatula. Pour 1 cup of water in the pot and insert the trivet. Lower the baking dish on the trivet.

Seal the lid, and cook for 25 minutes on High Pressure. Do a quick release. Transfer the pie to a serving platter. Refrigerate overnight before serving.

Warm Winter Apple Compote

Servings: 8 | Prep + Cook Time: 35 minutes

INGREDIENTS

1 lb fresh figs
7 oz Turkish figs
7 oz fresh cherries
7 oz plums
3.5 oz raisins
3 large apples, chopped

3 tbsp cornstarch
1 tsp cinnamon, ground
1 tbsp cloves
1 cup sugar
1 lemon, juiced
3 cups water

DIRECTIONS

Combine all ingredients in the instant pot. Seal the lid and cook for 30 minutes on High ´pressure. Release the pressure naturally, for 10 minutes. Store in big jars.

Vanilla Apple Tart

Servings: 6 | Prep + Cook Time: 30 minutes

INGREDIENTS

2 lb apples, cubed
¼ cup sugar
¼ cup breadcrumbs
2 tsp cinnamon, ground
3 tbsp freshly squeezed lemon juice

1 tsp vanilla sugar
¼ tbsp oil
1 egg, beaten
¼ cup all-purpose flour
Pie dough

DIRECTIONS

Combine breadcrumbs, vanilla sugar, granulated sugar, apples, and cinnamon, in a bowl. On a lightly floured surface, roll out the pie dough making 2 circle-shaped crusts.

Grease a baking sheet with cooking spray, and place one pie crust in it.

Spoon the apple mixture on top, and cover with the remaining crust. Seal by crimping edges and brush with beaten egg. Pour 1 cup of water in the instant pot and lay the trivet. Lower the baking sheet on the trivet. Seal the lid, and cook on High Pressure for 20 minutes. Do a quick release and serve chilled.

Chocolate & Banana Squares

Servings: 6 | Prep + Cook Time: 25 minutes

INGREDIENTS

½ cup Butter
3 Bananas
2 tbsp Cocoa Powder

1 ½ cups Water
Cooking spray, to grease

DIRECTIONS

Place the bananas and almond butter in a bowl and mash finely with a fork. Add the cocoa powder and stir until well combined. Grease a baking dish that fits into the pressure cooker.

Pour the banana and almond butter into the dish. Pour the water in the pressure cooker and lower the trivet. Place the baking dish on top of the trivet and seal the lid. Select Pressure Cook for 15 minutes at High pressure. When it goes off, do a quick release. Let cool for a few minutes before cutting into squares.

Yogurt Cake with Chocolate Glaze

Servings: 12 | Prep + Cook Time: 35 minutes

INGREDIENTS

3 cups yogurt
3 cups flour
2 cups granulated sugar
1 cup oil

2 tsp baking soda
3 tbsp cocoa, unsweetened
1 cup water

For the glaze:

7 oz dark chocolate
10 tbsp sugar

10 tbsp milk
5 oz butter, unsalted

DIRECTIONS

In a bowl, combine yogurt, flour, sugar, oil, baking soda, and cocoa. Beat well with an electric mixer. Transfer a mixture to a large springform pan.

Wrap the pan in foil. Insert a trivet in the instant pot. Pour in water, and place the pan on top. Seal the lid and cook for 30 minutes on High Pressure.

Do a quick release, remove the springform pan and unwrap. Chill well.

Meanwhile, melt the chocolate in a microwave. Transfer to a bowl, and whisk in butter, milk, and sugar. Beat well with a mixer and pour the mixture over the cake. Refrigerate for at least two hours before serving.

Savoury Lemon Dessert

Servings: 10 | Prep + Cook Time: 25 minutes

INGREDIENTS

2 eggs
2 cups sugar
2 cups vegetable oil

½ cup all-purpose flour
1 tsp baking powder

Lemon Topping:

4 cups sugar
5 cups water
1 cup freshly squeezed lemon juice

1 tbsp lemon zest
1 whole lemon, sliced

DIRECTIONS

In a bowl, combine eggs, sugar, oil, and baking powder. Gradually add flour until the mixture is thick and lightly sticky. Shape balls with hands, and flatten them to half-inch thick.

Place in a baking pan that fits in the instant pot. Pour 2 cups of water, insert the trivet and lower the pan onto the trivet. Cover the pan with foil and seal the lid. Cook on High Pressure for 20 minutes.

Do a quick release and remove the pan and foil. Cool to room temperature.

Add the remaining sugar, water, lemon juice, lemon zest, and lemon slices in the instant pot. Press Sauté and cook until the sugar dissolves. Pour the hot topping over the chilled dessert. Serve chilled.

Honey Crema Catalana

Servings: 4 | Prep + Cook Time: 15 minutes

INGREDIENTS

5 cups heavy cream
8 egg yolks
1 cup honey
4 tbsp sugar

1 tsp cinnamon
1 vanilla extract
¼ tsp salt
1 cup water

DIRECTIONS

In a bowl, combine heavy cream, egg yolks, vanilla, cinnamon, and honey. Beat well with an electric mixer. Pour the mixture into 4 ramekins. Set aside.

Pour water in the pot and insert the trivet. Lower the ramekins on top. Seal the lid, and cook for 10 minutes on High Pressure. Do a quick pressure release. Remove the ramekins from the pot and add a tablespoon of sugar in each ramekin. Burn evenly with a culinary torch until brown. Chill well and serve.

Marble Cherry Cake

Servings: 6 | Prep + Cook Time: 30 minutes

INGREDIENTS

1 cup flour
1 ½ tsp baking powder
1 tbsp powdered stevia
½ tsp salt
1 tsp cherry extract

3 tbsp butter, softened
3 eggs
¼ cup cocoa powder
¼ cup heavy cream

DIRECTIONS

Combine all dry ingredients, except cocoa in a bowl. Mix well to combine and add eggs, one at the time. Beat well with a dough hook attachment for one minute. Add sour cream, butter, and cherry extract.

Continue to beat for 3 more minutes. Divide the mixture in half and add cocoa powder in one-half of the mixture. Pour the light batter into a greased baking dish. Drizzle with cocoa dough to create a nice marble pattern.

Pour in one cup of water and insert the trivet. Lower the baking dish on top. Seal the lid and cook for 20 minutes on High Pressure. Release the pressure naturally, for about 10 minutes. Let it cool for a while and transfer to a serving plate.

Simple Apricot Dessert

Servings: 8 | Prep + Cook Time: 40 minutes

INGREDIENTS

2 lb fresh apricots, rinsed, drained
1 lb sugar
2 tbsp lemon zest

1 tsp ground nutmeg
10 cups water

DIRECTIONS

Add apricots, sugar, water, nutmeg, and lemon zest. Cook, stirring occasionally, until half of the water evaporates, on Sauté. Press Cancel, and transfer the apricots and the remaining liquid into glass jars. Let cool and close the lids. Refrigerate overnight before use.

Stewed Plums with Almond Flakes

Servings: 10 | Prep + Cook Time: 20 minutes

INGREDIENTS

6 lb sweet ripe plums, pits removed and halved
2 cups white sugar

1 cup almonds, flaked

DIRECTIONS

Drizzle the plums with sugar. Toss to coat. Let it stand for about 1 hour to allow plums to soak up the sugar.

Transfer the plum mixture to the instant pot and pour 1 cup of water. Seal the lid and cook on High Pressure for 30 minutes. Allow the Pressure to release naturally, for 10 minutes. Serve topped with almond flakes.

Vanilla & Walnut Cake

Servings: 8 | Prep + Cook Time: 15 minutes

INGREDIENTS

3 standard cake crusts
½ cup vanilla pudding powder
¼ cup granulated sugar

4 cups milk
1 (10.5oz) box chocolate chips
¼ cup walnuts, minced

DIRECTIONS

Combine vanilla powder, sugar and milk in the inner pot. Cook until the pudding thickens, stirring constantly, on Sauté. Remove from the steel pot.

Place one crust onto a springform pan. Pour half of the pudding and sprinkle with minced walnuts and chocolate chips. Cover with another crust and repeat the process. Finish with the final crust and wrap in foil.

Insert the trivet, pour in 1 cup of water, and place springform pan on top. Seal the lid and cook for 10 minutes on High Pressure. Do a quick release. Refrigerate overnight.

Vanilla Sweet Tortillas

Servings: 6 | Prep + Cook Time: 20 minutes

INGREDIENTS

2 medium-sized bananas, mashed
1 ¼ cup milk
2 eggs
1 ½ cups rolled oats
1 ½ tsp baking powder

1 tsp vanilla extract
2 tsp coconut oil
1 tbsp honey
¼ tsp salt
Non-fat cooking spray

DIRECTIONS

Combine the ingredients in a blender and pulse until a completely smooth batter. Grease the inner pot with cooking spray. Spread 1 spoon batter at the bottom.

Cook for 2 minutes, on Sauté mode, flip the crepe and cook for another minute. Repeat the process with the remaining batter. Serve immediately.

Pumpkin & Walnut Sweet Rolls

Servings: 8 | Prep + Cook Time: 30 minutes

INGREDIENTS

2 cups pumpkin puree
1 tsp vanilla extract
2 cups Greek yogurt
2 eggs

2 tbsp brown sugar
2 tbsp unsalted butter, softened
2 puff pastry sheets
1 cup walnuts, chopped

DIRECTIONS

In a bowl, mix yogurt with vanilla extract until completely smooth; set aside.

Unfold the pastry and cut each sheet into 4-inch x 7-inch pieces and brush with half of the beaten eggs. Place approximately 2 tbsp of pumpkin puree, and 2 tbsp of the yogurt mixture at the middle of each pastry, sprinkle with walnuts.

Fold the sheets and brush with the remaining eggs. Cut the surface with a sharp knife and gently place each strudel into an oiled baking dish.

Pour 1 cup of water in the pot and insert the trivet. Place the pan on top. Seal the lid and cook for 25 minutes on High Pressure.

Release the pressure naturally, for about 10 minutes. Let it chill for 10 minutes. Carefully Transfer the strudels to a serving plate.

Cinnamon & Lemon Apples

Servings: 2 | Prep + Cook Time: 13 minutes

INGREDIENTS

2 Apples, peeled and cut into wedges
½ cup Lemon Juice
½ tsp Cinnamon

1 tbsp Butter
1 cup Water

DIRECTIONS

Combine lemon juice and water in the pressure cooker. Place the apple wedges in the steaming basket and lower the basket into the cooker. Seal the lid, select the Pressure Cook for 3 minutes at High.

Release the pressure quickly. Open the lid and remove the steaming basket. Transfer the apple wedges to a bowl. Drizzle with almond butter and sprinkle with cinnamon.

Made in the USA
Coppell, TX
24 October 2021